Atlantic Currents II

Connecting Cork & Lowell

Atlantic Currents II

Connecting Cork & Lowell

Prose & Poetry

Edited by Paul Marion & John Wooding

A Project of Cork Learning City and Lowell: City of Learning

Loom Press
Amesbury, Massachusetts
2022

Atlantic Currents II: Connecting Cork & Lowell
Edited by Paul Marion and John Wooding

ISBN 978-0-931507-31-1

First edition
Printed in the USA

Book design: Joseph Marion
Text set in Helvetica Neue & Lyon
Printer: Versa Press
Cover images: Jason Murphy, Rosemary Noon

Loom Press
15 Atlantic View
Amesbury, Massachusetts 01913
www.loompress.com
info@loompress.com

Thank you to the Independent Alumni Association of the University of Massachusetts, Lowell, and University College Cork President's Office for generous support for this project.

Contents

Preface

It is with great pleasure that we present this collection of prose and poetry written by students and alumni of our two institutions.

This book is a sequel to *Atlantic Currents: Connecting Cork and Lowell* that presented the writing and creativity of the people of Cork and Lowell. The first *Atlantic Currents* landed on both sides of the ocean almost exactly as the Covid curtain came down on our societies. While its arrival was somewhat muted due to the virus, the collection of writing helped connect our two cities is a fresh way during the long lockdown. Writers associated with Cork and Lowell, and readers in both places, could open the book and be in touch through the power of words.

The new volume emphasizes the work of our current and former students, showcasing their imagination and creativity. It contains the results of a writing prize competition aimed at soliciting the best from our two campus communities. We congratulate all the authors for their success in what was a very competitive process.

Not only does this work illustrate the talents of our students and alumni, but it also celebrates and deepens the bond between our two campuses and their home cities. Such a partnership underlies our commonality, our commitment to excellence, and our respect for all our students and alumni.

This unique endeavor is not just about the creative process, it also demonstrates the importance of connection and collaboration between countries and people. The stories and poems in this anthology bring lively voices with ideas and emotions, beliefs and passion, to the printed page—some of the writers being published for the first time. This book makes a bold statement about the value of the creative process and the education of our people in institutions like ours.

Atlantic Currents II: Connecting Cork and Lowell offers intriguing stories and beautiful poems, which are a credit to their authors. We are delighted to welcome you to this collection. Enjoy!

Jacqueline Moloney, Chancellor
University of Massachusetts, Lowell

John O'Halloran, President
University College Cork

Foreword

There is an enduring connection between the people of Ireland and the United States anchored in the lives of millions of Irish immigrants who crossed the Atlantic Ocean in the 19th and 20th centuries. They and their descendants made an immense contribution to their adopted country. They also retained an affection for their Irish heritage and for their ancestral homeland. That connection is especially strong between Massachusetts and County Cork, which is why we are delighted to welcome the publication of this volume connecting the campuses of two great educational institutions and their respective cities.

As we work on the continued deepening of connections and engagement between our two countries, it is with pleasure that we celebrate this collection of prose and poetry written by students and alumni of the University of Massachusetts, Lowell and University College Cork.

These pages contain fine work by writers from both our shores. This collection illuminates the lives, experiences, and emotions of people from our two deeply-connected nations. It adds to the already deep and diverse cultural affinities between our two countries.

We congratulate the winners of this writing competition and thank all those who supported and organized this valuable work.

We are more than happy to applaud this partnership and the creative activity it illustrates and promotes.

With our best wishes/le meas mór,

Ambassador Daniel Mulhall,
Irish Ambassador to the United States

Ambassador Claire Cronin,
United States Ambassador to Ireland

Introduction

This companion volume to *Atlantic Currents: Connecting Cork and Lowell* is, like its predecessor, a product of Cork Learning City and Lowell: City of Learning. Continuing our relationship with Cork, Ireland, we organized a writing competition to solicit prose and poetry from the students and alumni of the University of Massachusetts, Lowell, and University College Cork. Both universities are critical to the vibrancy of their respective cities. We decided that one way to showcase what these institutions create was to publish the best writing from their former and current students.

The competition was designed to be as accessible as possible, and we encouraged submissions that spoke of personal learning experiences and their impact, irrespective of whether they occurred in a traditional classroom or in unique and unusual circumstances. The main goals were to get the creative juices flowing, provide recognition, and to promise the publication for our writers' efforts. The results are before you now.

At its core, the concept of a learning city recognizes that understanding, inquiry, curiosity, and knowledge occur in many places and in many formats. In *Atlantic Currents: Connecting Cork and Lowell* we purposely focused on giving voice to people who lived in or who were from these two cities. In so doing, we promoted the idea that skills and insights, thoughtful observations, and creativity exist outside of traditional learning institutions—in classrooms without walls. In this collection we mined the knowledge and skills of students and alumni of two universities. This was a means to connect the threads of the two campuses and to build on the partnerships that have developed.

We could not have done this work without the help of many people and institutions. The entire project would not have happened if not for a very generous grant from the Independent Alumni Association of the University of Massachusetts, Lowell. We are indebted to the Association for this support. We would especially like to thank Margaret Shanahan, the Executive Director, for her tireless effort and encouragement.

We would also like to thank the University of Massachusetts and its staff and faculty for helping us promote the project and Chancellor Jacqueline Moloney for her support. We are indebted in the same way to University College Cork. Without a generous donation from the office of President John O'Halloran this project could never have been fully completed. Both institutions helped us form a partnership.

Denis Barrett, Cork Learning City Coordinator and dear friend and colleague, helped make many of our connections in Cork and has always been an irreplaceable supporter of this work. Tina Neylon of Cork (co-editor of our previous volume) gave us advice and was one of our judges for the competition.

Patricia Looney, Director of Cork Public Libraries, provided insight and served as our second Cork-based judge. We thank her.

In Lowell, Sarah Alcott Anderson and David Daniel did an amazing job reviewing submissions and making difficult choice. We thank them for their time and dedication.

—Paul Marion and John Wooding

Margaret O'Driscoll

Moondancing in the Bay of Biscay

Crossing the Bay of Biscay presents a challenge for all yachtsmen and women. It is a notoriously unpredictable area as sea conditions can change at very short notice turning a slow lazy swell into sharp breaking waves. Those who have sailed it are granted a quiet respect from their fellow sailors. I was reluctantly about to join that elite group early one April, however it was not an accolade I had ever even remotely thought about acquiring.

My husband Donal and I were sailing *Ré Shuanta* our forty-one-foot Halberg Rassey ketch from Bayona in the north of Spain, to our home port of East Ferry in Cork Harbour. Six hundred and eleven nautical miles lay ahead, a passage that would take up to four days and nights, possibly longer if the weather turned foul and the wind became a gale. However, we were under a time pressure to set off as we both had to return to work. The forecast was fair but there was the possibility that we might encounter some strong wind as we sailed further north. This was a small weather window, and we had to make the most of it. I was not relishing the hours that lay ahead.

The two days before our trip were busy with several trips to the supermarket for stores, then I cooked some dinners which were flat packed in the fridge ready to be reheated and eaten straight from the pot. Nuts, biscuits, and snacks were stored in the treats box to keep up our spirits on the night watch. Donal topped up the fresh water and fuel tanks, did a final check on the engine, made sure everything was stowed and secured, we were as ready as we could be. On the night before a sea passage apprehension builds, an awareness of all that is at stake over the following days, but this disappears the moment you stow the shorelines and fenders and head to sea. Action takes over.

As dawn was breaking on that sunny April morning we cast

off, then steamed out to Point De Silbeiro, four-and-a-half miles northwest of the harbour, brought her head into the wind to raise the main sail, unfurled the genoa in the gentle breeze and set her on a course of 360 degrees, straight north. This would keep us clear of Cape Finisterre. After we cleared the land we set up our watch system, three hours on, three off, which were mostly spent catching up on sleep. It always takes me a while to settle into the rhythm of the swell as the boat lifts and dips, my stomach not always matching the same rhythm. When I first started sailing I suffered badly from sea sickness and had to spend the entire time lying down so I was of no help as crew. For this trip I had mentally convinced myself that I couldn't afford to feel unwell as I had to cover my watch to allow the skipper some rest.

The boat was revelling in the conditions, her sails filled, making a steady six knots without being too heeled over. Literally translated the name *Ré Shuanta* means "the calm way, the peaceful way." We always referred to her as being "sea kindly," due to her weight and long keel she was not tossed about as much as lighter boats. The name is also connected to Cape Clear Island in West Cork where Donal grew up. Their house looked out on the rock known as Bird Island, and between this rock and the shore there is always a stretch of calm water used by the ferry and local boats when storms rage across Roaring Water Bay. While my limited sea experience only involved lazy swimming or spending hours fishing off the end of a pier in the hope of catching a mackerel, Donal could read the sea; he had spent all his life dealing with it in one way or other. He had seen enough suns rise and set on the ocean so they no longer excited him, whereas for me it is always a mystical experience to observe that golden chariot appearing from the deep. That moment never failed to inspire me.

When dark settles over the ocean everything seems different, and it can be a lonely space. I steer by hand, keeping an eye on the compass, holding the boat on track. Every thirty minutes or so I put her on auto pilot, record our position in the log, keep a sharp look out for the lights of any other vessels in case we were on a collision course. However, on a clear night it's a magical world, the sky full of stars, and when you're really lucky, a shooting star disappearing into the ocean. My mother believed that whenever a shooting star travelled across the sky, a soul was on its way to heaven. Then my eye wanders to the white brightness on the road known as The Milky Way, weaving like a magic path. To pass the time I search for the constellations that are familiar. Firstly, to ground myself, I scan for my old reliable, The Plough. Seven stars spread across the sky, four define a body or bowl, and three a handle or head. I draw an imaginary line between the two pointer stars and continue to the first bright star I encounter, mighty Polaris, the North Star. It always directs the sailor true north, but presents itself as almost inconsequential, surrounded by so many others that are brighter. Feeling totally alone in a complete circle of ocean that stretches all the way to the horizon, is almost like sailing under an upside-down basin. That's when I start to sing, belting it out at the top of my voice. Always the same song surfacing, "Moondance."

Immediately, I am transported back to Cotter's Garden on Cape Clear during the previous summer. It is a warm July afternoon, a group of us are seated around a table savouring slow lazy drinks. Sally, a young girl who is working in the bar for the summer months, is strumming her guitar and singing her favourite songs. My eyes drift over the low wall to the harbor and the activity happening there, yachts and small boats arriving to spend a few hours, enjoy a swim, ramble up the hill for a drink before heading back to the mainland again. Locals driving out the pier to collect boxes of groceries, bags of fertilizer, spare parts for a tractor, all brought to the island by ferry, and left on the pier for collection. Suddenly, I am held captive by the words of a new song, a lilting melody, lyrical notes that catch at me and will not let go. After our applause has subsided, I ask Sally about the song and who had recorded it. "Moondance" by Van Morrison, a song of love and yearning for the beloved. I couldn't wait to get to You Tube and make it my own which I did as soon as I returned home and had enjoyed singing it since then in the car or when cooking the dinner.

"It's a marvelous night for a moondance, with the stars up above in your eyes." An exhilarating inhibition, the boat my stage, while I bogey and sway caressing the steering wheel. "And all the soft moonlight seems to shine in your blush." On and on I go like a recording on a loop, no other song ever felt so right for the setting, the motion of the boat under me, the audience above winking in time. "And when I touch you, you just tremble inside . . . ." I was the one trembling inside, realising how vast the ocean appeared, and how we were such a minuscule dot on its surface. Singing always dissolved my sense of loneliness. Our watches passed and disappeared one into the other, and we made steady progress northwards, but our holiday was almost over.

Since we departed Bayona Donal had been regularly tuning in to the BBC Shipping Forecast and recording it in our log. He would then mark the position of the centre of the low pressure that was approaching on our chart. On the third night of our passage, the wind was set to strengthen from the northwest, with gusts of up to force seven. This would last for the following twelve hours and bring a steep sea. It did not disappoint and arrived as scheduled, we were close hauled and sail motoring with the sail area reduced. The increasing swell pitched us from side-to-side, but the boat could handle these conditions better than myself. The wind roared through my head; my stomach performed summersaults. It felt like I was being tossed around inside the drum of a washing machine cycle. I was terrified.

I found it difficult to get from the bunk to the cockpit to relieve Donal when my watch was due. It took me a while to adjust my eyes to the conditions, all was gloomy and blustery. I felt myself wrapped in its cloak of isolation, a lone sentinel, all senses alert, eagle-eyed. I sat staring at the spray that was reflected in our navigation lights as they briefly illuminated the swell. The boat creaked and groaned, banging into the trough, I imagined everything below deck being smashed and thrown about. I trusted the skipper had succeeded in wedging himself into the bunk and was able to sleep. I scrolled out from our position on the chart plotter which read, 45° 28.5'N, 09°43.4'W. We were two hundred miles from the coast of France, and it was also two hundred miles to the south coast of Ireland, so there was no option for respite only to plough on. I clung on to that steering wheel, every muscle screaming, holding our compass course, willing us homewards.

That was when I began to summon the dolphins. If I had a large white conch I would have invited them with resonant notes across the waves, instead from deep inside me I beseeched them to come and keep me company. I scanned the water around the hull by the cockpit, hoping and patiently waiting. I was in need of rescuing just like Arion had been rescued when he was drowning. His lungs ready to burst, he felt himself being pushed upwards, surging through the water, he was on the back of a dolphin and he could breathe. Eventually he was landed safely ashore in the Gulf of Corinth. Still no sign of my spirit animals, twice more I recorded our position in the log, tiredness and cold seeping through my bones. Then I spotted them, a pod of dolphins cavorting, riding the light in the water, darting across under the hull, jumping clean out of the waves. Instantly I had the boat on auto, clipped on my harness, heading up on the high side of the deck to lie flat as close to the edge of her bow as I was able to wriggle, shouting, cheering, and clapping my hands. They are considered to be lucky and a symbol of protection, and I certainly believed that to be the case.

Swimming on their backs, frolicking across her bow, their eyes on the sides of their heads interlocking with mine, I became Arion gamboling and rollicking alongside these magnificent creatures. I could hear their squeaks and clicks and I sent my own in reply, "Can I just have one more moondance with you my love," anything to keep them with me, to discourage their taking off back across the vastness of that lonely sea. I was transformed, when finally, they soared off over the waves, diving in unison. I reckoned they had spent almost a quarter of an hour keeping watch with me. My positive energy had been restored. I forgot about the cold, the rain that had found its way down inside my oilskin, where even my neck towel was wet, didn't figure any more. The remainder of my watch floated along until it was time to wake my relief. When Donal took over, I crawled down below, jammed myself into the warm bunk he had just vacated, instantly exhaustion took over. Winking images of Arion and his rescuer, the dolphin, forever now the constellation Delphinus, drifted around my dreaming. The magical kinship that exists between dolphin and mankind.

The swell eased over the following day and night, and we continued to plough our way north until we picked up the gas platforms which are approximately twenty miles south of Cork Harbour. Then the land slowly presented itself rising from the sea, and I began to tidy the mess in the saloon and galley, as we counted down the last miles to Roches Point, the lighthouse at the entrance. Once we secured the lines ashore my emotions coasted between elation and anti-climax all at the same time. After we had finished cleaning the boat, we decided to sleep on board for one more night as we were reluctant to abandon her. That evening I sat savouring a mug of tea, enjoying the stillness and the thrill of setting the mug down without it rolling away. The water ironed flat as a sheet, not even a wrinkle, as if the sea was also resting.

My thoughts drifted back over the voyage. While I had felt terrified at times and ached where I never knew there were muscles, I had also felt energised and focused. Something had shifted inside; an inner flint had been forged. Because of that experience I realised that anything was possible if I really wanted to pursue it. I had faced down my inner fears and found a core resolve. I continued with my writing and started to believe in my own voice. I summoned those dolphins and sharpened that steel over the following years when rejection emails pinged for my poetry submissions and I continued steering my pen across the page. I remembered those seas and that endless pounding once more when walking through the gates of UCC to begin my Master's in Creative Writing, exactly fifty years to the date I had first dreamt of being a student there. When portfolio deadlines loomed and I struggled to reconnect to my muse, I dug deep and stayed on course knowing there was no turning back. I continue to summon those dolphins whenever storms threaten, knowing I can crest the waves and remain afloat.

Christine O'Connor

Annie's Bike, Brian Friel, and Translating Loss

There had been a death in the family, a cousin in Galway. Although Anne was ninety-six, it was unexpected. She was the oldest living member of the Toolan family and was born in the same stone-walled cottage in Sligo that was once a home to my grandmother. On Valentine's Day in 1953, she married Thomas Diskin, and settled on a farm in Galway where together they raised three children. She was tall, thin, and athletic, and even rode a bike well into her late eighties. For me, Annie was the one who bore a striking resemblance to my grandmother, and as such, was a constant reminder that we are all part of something greater than ourselves.

On the morning of her passing I remember imagining how different the kitchen in Corohan must have seemed without her. I thought of her chair by the cook-stove, suddenly unoccupied as the ten o'clock death notices played on Midwest radio: "Annie Diskin (née Toolan) Corohan, Dunmore, Galway, formerly Meelroe, Gurteen, Sligo, in her ninety-seventh year after a brief illness, predeceased by her much-loved husband Tom, deeply regretted by her loving family, son Billy, daughters Marie and Anne, sister Teresa and her extended family. RIP."I went "home," as the Irish say, that November for Annie's Month's Mind Mass. I felt I owed much to her. At a time when our family stateside was growing smaller, it was Annie and other relations in Ireland who made those gone feel close again. Planes can be great contemplative spaces, and hurling through the night sky I thought of what my grandmother often said of those gone: "I suppose they're up in heaven with Mini and Maggie, Nora and Nell, Briggie and Ger; have'n a grand time for themselves . . . if there is such a place." Such thoughts of heaven and the reunion of souls lingered until the morning light crept behind the window shade. As the plane descended, I could see the small trails of smoke circling out of the chimneys below and a nation slowly waking.In Galway I attended Annie's Mass, and not far from the church visited the graveyard. Her stone was rain-soaked and topped with a Celtic cross. Within the cross at each end were decorative knots. The knots have no beginning or end, and as such represent the pre-Christian belief in the interconnectedness of life and the eternity of this world to the next. The knots each have three points, simultaneously representing the Christian belief in the Trinity. There is sometimes great meaning in the smallest of things.Back at the house, I joined others for sandwiches and tea and cake in a crowded room of handshakes and familiar voices. Black-and-white photos of Annie posing in front of an old Morris Minor, at weddings and graduations, and even one in the field milking a cow, were spread across the kitchen table. It was a sad time, made even more so with that bit of melancholy and nostalgia that November brings. No longer, I thought, would I pack a gift from America for her or feel the grip of her hand as I entered the kitchen; no longer would I hear the voice that was so like my grandmother's. Sadness, sympathy, and depth of loss are subjects not easily translated to others. Are there words for all we feel?Following the services, I left for a brief getaway to Donegal with Teresa, Annie's younger sister, and Marie, Annie's daughter. Under a blue sky, in a color they just don't make in America, we packed the car and prepared to put some miles between us and that little graveyard in Corahan. If only grief could be so easily left behind.We planned to spend a few days at Harvey's Point in Donegal town, and booked a family suite at an off-season, mid-week special. Situated on the shores of Lough Eske and surrounded by the Blue Mountains, the hotel is often ranked number one in Ireland. Our first Donegal stop was in Glenties to find the grave of playwright Brian Friel. It was just the year before, also in October, that Friel was laid to rest. After a bit of searching, we found it, high on a hilltop overlooking what became the fictional valley of Baile Beag. It's Irish for "small village," but in English its meaning is lost. In his play *Translations*, Friel explored such limitations and complexities of language: "It is not the literal past that shapes us ... but images of the past embodied in language," he wrote.

During our stay, we stood over the cliffs at Slieve League, the steepest in all of Europe; drove to the farthest point in Ireland, Malin Head; ate cheese sandwiches in Glenveagh National Park, and while visiting the Castle there, discussed the mysterious disappearance of Professor Porter. He sailed to Inishbofin one fine morning, never to be seen again. At night we sat before one of the hotel's many open fires, laid out brochures and discussed the next day's excursion. Each evening we'd order a warm glass of milk for Teresa and play cards in our room until it was time for bed. On our last morning, we watched the sun rise over Locke Eske. The earth and sky so mirrored each other, it was hard to tell where one ended and the other began.

On our way home, we decided on an impromptu stop at the National Museum of Country Life as we were passing through Mayo. It's a museum dedicated to the folklife of rural Ireland; and I was struck by the everyday things I happened upon there: the variety of St. Brigid crosses; a piano with sheet music from the West of Sligo; carved turnips preserved from long ago Samhain nights; a Singer sewing machine; handwoven baskets, and hanging on the wall, a vintage black Raleigh bike. I snapped some pictures.

As an American, the museum brought a sense of familiarity I wasn't expecting. Its exhibits were more than a connection to the past; they were a connection to those of the past. My grandparents were from the West of Ireland. Walking by the displays I was reminded of the hook-rug my grandmother made from clothing scraps, the black-beaded rosary that hung from her bed post, and the kitchen knife that my grandfather used to peel an apple in one long strip. These were objects of everyday life; but to museumgoers they were also charged with personal meaning and memory. This unromantic celebration of the ordinary moved me in a way our travels hadn't.

The word museum comes from the ancient Greek, *mouseion*,

which means a place dedicated to the muses. In many ways the objects they hold are not just meant to be seen, but to communicate and inspire. I recalled reading that when the Japanese first encountered Western museums, they had difficulty finding a comparable word for such places. Eventually they settled on *hakubutsukan*, meaning "a house of extensive things." It is a word that translates well for this museum in Mayo, where everyday objects are collected and valued.

"We still have my mother's bike in the barn," said my cousin Marie as we got back into the car.

"The one she'd ride a hundred miles to Sligo?"

"Yes Chris, the very one."

Soon after we arrived back, I was in the barn, passing the pile of turf, the discarded shovels, hay rakes, and empty cans of paint; and then I found it, cobwebbed and a bit buried: Annie's bike. It was rusty in spots and the tires needed air. It was a classic black enamel Raleigh, probably from the eighties, with a rack on the back and a wide saddle. I pulled it out and rolled it across the field to the house.

With a bucket of soap and water I washed the frame, and let it dry in the sun. I pumped the tires and tightened the brakes. All the while, I thought of Annie, sailing along the road to Garrafrauns or Milltown. I imagined copies of the *Independent* or the *Tuam Herald* tied to the bike-rack, their corners flapping in the wind. Staples like tea and flour, butter and jam, and even the occasional lotto ticket were all transported with this bike. Wiping the front reflector, I imagined the many times it must have glowed in the dusk of autumn evenings.

Once everything appeared in working order, I gripped the handlebars and slowly rode down the drive onto the same stretch of road Annie took. Stonewalls and farmed land, generations old, bordered my path as I felt my hold on the present loosen. I passed the empty, half-thatched cottage where once the Diskins lived; passed the fairy mound in one of Annie's former fields, and finally passed the graveyard where she now rests with her husband Tom beneath a most comforting thought: *In Iothliann Dé*

Go Dtugtar Sinn (We Are Gathered in the Haggard of the Lord). That autumn's descending sun must have caught the bike's red reflectors as they spun round, like the universe itself. My lungs filled with the sweet smell of hay, and everywhere I looked was bathed in a golden light. It seemed for at least a moment, that there was such a place as heaven.

As I pulled back in the driveway, her son Bill hollered out the window: "For a moment I thought the old lady herself was back."

Laughter, a sign that we are all right. Parking the Raleigh up against the house I noticed something. I pulled out my phone and with a single finger scanned until I came upon the photo of the bike hanging at the Museum of Country Life. It was exactly the same: the same color, saddle, handlebars, and bike-rack. Both the one on display and the one before me filled me with feelings of love and loss, but mainly the former. Sitting atop that bike, I felt connected to Annie. Sometimes objects can speak to us in ways words can't because they tell us things that are to be felt rather than said. Maybe we are, as Friel claimed, shaped by the images of the past, and maybe an old Raleigh can help express our love of those gone, in a language far richer than our own.

Pat Brett

Things I Would Have Told You in the Canteen

In the beginning.
I'm lucky. I am an introvert, I have a job that I can do from home, I have a garden to patrol, I've recently upgraded my broadband . . . and I have plenty of toilet roll. I can do this. Think of all the time I'll have to tackle the things I've long-fingered. I'll get fit, too, apparently, with all that saved commuting time converted to exercise.

Don't forget to remember me.
My cocooning mother has spent some time rooting out old photos, including an old school class picture. I could only remember about half of the names, with a few more on the tip of my tongue but just not there . . . which has me wondering whether we'll all remember each other's names when we meet in the office or on the street when this is all over! Cue awkward moments. Best keep the cameras on for any meetings you have.

Random thoughts.
For some reason, as we run out of new things to talk about, forming coherent narratives about anything seems harder. My brain is turning into a twitter account; my internal algorithm generating random brief musings that are not all worthy of, or suitable for, public consumption: I feel like I'm in the movie *Room*; should I give my new under-the-windowsill spider pet a name? "Flattening the curve" is the phrase of the moment, but I'm just fattening my curves with comfort eating.

The novelty wears off.
Perceived wisdom is that this lockdown is ok for introverts. Not if the introvert has a partner and five kids. Not a moment alone.

Did I say I was lucky?

Locked down and locked out.
During a recent time-filling rummage in the garage I came across a vice grips, some masking tape and WD40. As any in-tune person knows, that's all you need to be a DIY emergency king. As my domestic contribution for the day, I confidently strode around the house, spraying WD40 into the many door hinges that had become more noticeably noisy during lockdown. The front door got particular attention as it had developed a loud groaning noise over time. Worried mice scurried toward the exits as word spread that the man was spraying oil into anything that might squeak. The exercise was a resounding success. The front door had never moved more smoothly or soundlessly.

Flash forward a week. Alone in the house as the school run was being done, mid-meeting online with some senior colleagues, the doorbell rang. Unexpectedly. I made my excuses, headed to the hallway, and opened the door to meet nothing and no one. My brain can still work fast at times, and I quickly deduced that the frustratingly inaccurate Eircode had sent a delivery man next door where he had asked the neighbour if he could pop through the hedge and drop off the package—which he did before scarpering at pace. The package was actually early and was a rare treat for myself—needing, as I did, some Health & Well Being solace this time of year.

Looking down at the sizeable enough package left to the side of the door, my manual handling training kicked in . . . I had enough on my plate this month without putting my back out. I took a step forward, bent down (knees not back) and, as I rose and turned, heard the quiet click of the door that had silently taken revenge for all the years of being unceremoniously banged shut. A quick audit confirmed that I had no key, no phone, no windows were open, and I had no knowledge of whether the school run was a quick turnaround or just the first stop on a morning offsite.

On the bright side of my internal feedback framework, I was fully clothed, it was not raining, the package was a 627-page book that could pass the time, and I was sure my colleagues would soon be ringing the emergency services when my unexplained disappearance and non-answering of the phone went on too long and their ladder of inference had me in a dire situation.

Skipping a few chapters (including how I managed to position myself at my neighbour's door asking for a message to be relayed whilst standing in a way that hid my indoor footwear from view, all under the guise of being physically distant; thanks Covid), making a long story short because we're all busy . . . the wait was not too long and I re-joined the meeting after twenty minutes to find my colleagues ploughing through the agenda like a dispassionate buffalo herd that has lost a member to a predator, but is just getting on with eating grass as if nothing has happened.

My "to do" list has grown—put an emergency key somewhere, trim the gap in the hedge so no one loses an eye, and figure out how to fix the Eircode database. On balance, it's all good—
better miss some of a meeting than have a bad back for a week. Once upon a time this could have ruined my day. Now it's an adventure and a tale to tell.

The Garden of Adventure.
I ended up crawling sniper-like in the garden today with heiress #3, after we first engaged in a Keystone Cop-like pursuit, to get a close-up snap of a lovely lilac butterfly, a type we have rarely seen. Mission having been accomplished, I googled it to learn that it's called the Common Blue Butterfly. Common? C'mon! After all that effort. Still, it passed a few minutes, and it can be counted as quality parenting time.

The belly crawling skills that I perfected during the pursuit of the common blue came in handy again a few days later. I've enjoyed watching various birds feed their young. Initially on purposeful flights across the garden to seek out some grubs, worms, or seeds, with a quick return to the same spot each time—a hidden nest the unseen but obvious destination—and later, wandering around pursued by loudly squawking fledglings who are often as big if not bigger than the weary parent. One such parent, a dedicated blackbird, has been hopping around near the garage, feeding two offspring. It wasn't looking too healthy though. In fact, it was clearly dying. I took it upon myself to dig up some worms, place them on a shovel, crawl toward the patient and let them rest within reach. Poor thing didn't have the energy to either eat them or fly away. It would have had a long night in the garden. Too many prowling cats. I didn't bother looking for it the next day.

There's been a murder.
I'm not one for watching the tv soaps . . . at least not since *Home & Away* was an after school-day distraction in a decade long ago featured in *Reeling in the Years*. For the past year, I have witnessed plenty of real-life action outside my window. The bird feeders have been a welcome diversion. One pair of visitors in recent months has been a couple of collared doves. Always together, dropping in a few times a day. Too big to balance and extract food from the feeders, they devour the inevitable mess left on the ground by the others. They look great as they swoop in, wings and tail out for a soft and graceful landing.

Last week, whilst checking out the nature camera in the corner of the garden, I spotted a scattering of grey feathers on the grass. Needless to say, and perhaps best for our younger viewers, whatever action took place was just outside the cameras range, but it looked like the tattered jacket of a pigeon. I thought no more about it for a couple of days, until the next workday in fact. As the laptop booted up, I saw a single collared dove arrive. No sign of his/ her partner. I'm no Poirot, but I figured the pigeon feathers must actually have been dove feathers and the small-headed dinosaur-descendent outside my window was now flying solo.

There's a song for every moment, and the one that came to mind is a recent Springsteen album-opener "One minute you're here . . . ." Even if you're in the majority that have not heard the song, you can guess the second line. Sombre moment.

Next morning, the newly single dove returned. A few seconds later, a second dove followed! All was right in the world again. For about five seconds—at which point one dove chased the other off and returned alone again. One step forward, two steps back. Looks like the two were not the original pair. They hadn't been the bickering type.

Later in the day my failure to implement a capture, tag, and release programme to assist identification of the original doves came back to haunt me as up to four doves turned up at one point. Maybe three were turning up for the funeral. Or maybe it was the original couple and two guests over for grub(s), outdoors of course. Who knows? The next morning it's back to two. I am going to assume the best and that the originals are back. Is it a happy ending? I don't know. But I choose to believe it is. For those two birds anyway.

Tiptoe through the tulips.
Sometime in late 2020 I purchased and sowed some bulbs randomly around the garden (yes, I'm part of the pandemic cliché). Even if all survived to bloom, I wouldn't be winning any competitions. The "green" in green-fingered in my world means novice rather than talented on such things. I keep sending pics to my sister—"Is that something I planted or a colourful weed?" Flash forward to March, and I start seeing some growth. Soccer with the kids, in addition to all the usual clauses about not kicking my ankles, now included the unfair demand that their blossoming talents extended to not hitting my flowers-to-be under pain of death, which was a bit harsh given that I had planted some in the middle of the pitch. The daily stroll outside my cell now included a walk-by, assessing progress. Two stalks in particular

kept my attention as they are in my eyeline through the window. As some colour began to appear, and reminding me that my plant-recognition talent lags behind my lockdown-acquired bird twitching skills and that I don't know everything even if I tell the kids I do, investigation confirmed that these were two tulips. In your face, Netherlands!

Things were looking up in early April; almost a foot tall and the flowers on the cusp of full blown fanfare. Until a frosty morning (outside, not inside, thankfully) and a quick glance brings a sigh and an R-rated muttering. Red is listing at forty-five degrees. Looks romantic as he is tilting toward Yellow, but he ain't gonna make it. The gap is too wide, albeit in line with the guidelines on the packet which I assume were written by the same nun who had the dancehall rule about being a foot apart for the slow set. This is not a show of affection, but the beginning of the end. One day after opening, like a rules-compliant hairdresser between lockdowns, Red is shutting down again.

Surprisingly, one hour later, as the sun re-conquered the garden, Red is back to within a degree of vertical. I guess that counts as a sprint in plant-time. Maybe it's a pace we could all do with once in a while. All was well in the world. Spring in the air, Summer coming. Until the dove who has gorged on the fat-ball I have left out on the bird feeder today, and whose welfare caused me some concern last week, does a fly-over and leaves a fertiliser deposit on top of Red. What doesn't kill the flower will make it stronger. Red and white. Up Cork!

Sorry, if I took you for granted.
My offspring returned to school this week. Awake at the crack of dawn on Monday, with each passing day they have slumbered a little longer as they tire from the return to a routine not kept since March. Collecting them on Day 1, I asked one pre-pubescent deep thinker how they got on and who they were sitting with. For full effect I'd need to convey his reflective tone as he gazed out the

window and responded matter-of-factly, but the written word, paraphrasing his response, will have to do.

I feel like the trauma of the birds-and-the-bees conversation is still a little away with this guy anyway. Not for the first time, the unconscious wisdom of youth got me thinking. The following day I logged in to read that we will continue to work remotely for at least the remainder of the year. Replacing the energy and buzz in our company generally, and in our team specifically, during the Halloween to Christmas period with a ground-floor window view of dreary weather and damp grass doesn't feel like a fair deal, but like every challenge put to this team, this one will be overcome too. One thing is for sure, when we do get back, I expect that we won't take the company of others for granted. Maybe any little "annoying" things about those we sit near won't seem like such a big deal anymore because, let's face it: as people go, the people in our team are "about the best of them." I wonder if other teams feel the same, or are we special?

I might be standing still, but nature is evolving.
I've been at the window so long now that I am witnessing Darwinian evolution in action. Birds that for months have been enthralled spectators as smaller or more agile feathered feeders mastered the balancing act required to gorge on my expensive seeds have grown tired of waiting for the fallen leftovers. The robin can jump up quickly a seize a beakful before flying off and, more impressively, the starlings now leap on board and curve their backs to allow their beaks line up with the access hole. Future generations may see curved-back starlings and wonder about the how and the why. I wonder if these future starlings will be able to impress with murmurations as fascinating as those that currently saturate social media and nature programmes.

To bee or not to bee.
I enjoy cutting the grass. It's a mindful hour. A bit less pleasant this time of year when the hundreds (thousands?) of buttercups

and daisies get mixed up with the wrong crowd and face being collateral damage during the necessary green cull. On a recent circuit I came upon a bee on his rounds, fully focused on his nectar gathering. He didn't spot me coming (opportunity for some extra-eyes or better hearing evolution). Being aware of the importance of bees to the survival of the human race, and in no particular rush to get back to doing nothing indoors, I paused and waited for him to finish rather than putting him in a bladed spin. I gave myself a pat on the back for being so environmentally aware. That bee may have been the tipping point. I even contemplated replacing our tiny vegetable patch with flowers next Summer.

An hour later and heir #2 seeks assistance—the football had been banished into the almost impenetrable bushes over the wall. Opportunities to be Hero Daddy are less frequent as the kids get older, so I put on my superhero gear (boots and old jacket, didn't bother with the machete) and in I went. Mission accomplished, I had commenced my exit when I felt a really sharp pain in my arm. Coming on the day I had read about false black widow spider bites putting people in intensive care in the sunny Southeast, my ever-ready ladder of inference had me in big trouble. Long story short, it wasn't a spider bite, it was a sting—one that left its mark for a few days. It hurt. And my empathy for nature was tested. Allow me a plot hole worthy of Dallas . . . maybe the bee I didn't shred was the one who stung me later. It's a big stretch. But it allows me to ponder . . . .

Stopping what we are doing, to do the right thing, might not be the easiest path sometimes (It might even hurt in the short term!) but it's still the right thing. Stepping up as leaders on anything is not the easy option. It is easier to look away and ignore what we see. This is particularly the case if we are busy. It can be easier to keep the momentum on the task at hand and not divert to address the thing we spot—the bee in the way of the mower. I wonder how many bees are in front of the mower that is the human race and will we ever slow down.

Let nature take its course.
Number 4 knows not to interrupt me when working with machinery, but today he wildly gesticulated for God knows how long before I noticed him. He had spotted a chick on the ground below a known nesting spot. After considerable ill-informed consideration, we decided a ladder should be scaled and the little fellow shoved back into bed. Having proudly shown my offspring how good and caring I was, we sat at a distance and watched a while. Hearts began to sink and reality began to dawn as we saw both parents in turn repeatedly arrive laden with worms, frantically search the ground where their chick had been last seen before swallowing and flying off. They were mere feet from the nest, but unable to register that their fledgling had reverted to nestling. Our hastily convened nature committee decided that we needed to retrieve the chick and return him to terra firma, but the initial shove into the nest was too good. He was out of reach. We continued to watch. At one point a haughty Garfield strolled past which gave us some solace—we had at least saved the chick from that fate. Not everything in the garden has had a happy ending this year, but thankfully a couple of tense hours later we finally witnessed a parent hop back into the nest. All was well again. For now. Is this why reporters don't interfere when embedded in traumatic situations? The fear of unintended consequences from good Samaritan attempts?

A glimpse of normality.
When I was a boy—black hair, no glasses, and thin as a pull-through for a rifle—my brother and I went to watch our father play indoor soccer in an inter-business league match. It was, quite frankly, one of the most traumatic hours of my young life. It was prison-rule stuff. Running battles between grown men a few feet from my perch on a bench. I worried that I'd be half-orphaned by full-time.

With that in mind, I was more than a little concerned when my eldest son asked to watch our Wednesday night soccer game . . . after a long lockdown layoff, and conscious of my aforementioned curve fattening, I was planning to ease my way back into things with a lot of pointing and shouting with only a little running. I was not ready for him to see through the cloak of invincibility that parents wear in their kids' eyes in their early years . . . but he really wanted to come along, so following some conditioning on what he might expect to see, he became the first spectator we've ever had. I hoped he'd take some learnings back to his own team.

Following a discreet "Don't embarrass me or traumatise him" request to my fellow players, we kicked off. I scored a goal. One box ticked. A couple of timely interventions followed . . . it was going well. Then I went over on my ankle. I hobbled around for a bit, gave him a thumb's up to let him know that this need not be a memory to bother him in the future, and made it to full-time relatively unscathed.

I asked later him for his impressions, expecting to hear about the clever positional play and good passing that we believe we exhibit each week. His response: "Well, it's not quite like watching Barcelona is it, ye seem to walk away from the ball a lot, and I get less time on the ball in my U11 matches." I also asked him who stood out as a good player. "The guy with the red boots." I have no idea which of the other thirteen players he meant. I never look at the shoes (eyes on the ball!).

His brutal honesty brought to mind five things. Firstly, giving feedback can be powerful. And how we give that feedback is equally important. (Kids—and some adults I guess—are great at the former, not too concerned about the latter). Secondly, getting an external view on performance is something that may take us out of our comfort zone, but can give us real insight and drive us on to better things. Uncomfortable as it can be, it will make us better. Thirdly, it's great to be back on the pitch. Fourthly, I apparently need red boots. I'll buy those when retail reopens.

Finally, it feels good to talk about something other than . . . you know what.

Pre match tension

The boss has scheduled a face-to-face meeting for a group of ten. With vaccine dose two imminent, I feel like the movie cop two days from retirement. I don't want to take a bullet at the finish line. I can't hide away forever. Time to fledge the nest. I am nervous. How are you?

Alan Egan

An Extraordinary Man

Maurice Desmond Hickey, the fifth of nine children, was born on June 11, 1915. His birthplace was the family home on Western Road in Cork city, just a skip and a jump away from the gates of University College Cork. On completing his secondary education, Maurice gained admission to that self-same place of learning and in 1941, at the age of twenty-six, he graduated with a degree in medicine. Not alone did he achieve first class honours, he won the Peel Memorial Prize as the outstanding UCC graduate that year, as well as the Pearson Medal in surgery. In addition, he was awarded the Blayney scholarship and bursary and went on to graduate with a Masters in Surgery (M.Ch.) in 1943.

Following his graduation Maurice trained in Nottingham General Hospital and Nottingham City Hospital. Here he met Dr. Mary Bourke, also from Cork, and they were married on August 23, 1945. This talented couple moved to London where Maurice became assistant surgeon in the London Chest Hospital to Thomas Holmes Sellors, the leading British thoracic of his generation, and for the next few years Maurice Hickey was at the then cutting edge (pun intended) of thoracic surgery and treatment of T.B.

At this stage, I note that I am referring to this exceptional man as "Maurice," despite the fact that for as long as I knew him I never addressed him as nothing other than "Mr. Hickey."

Fortuitously, or perhaps it was written in the stars, another remarkable man had just come to the fore in Irish health and political circles. This was Dr. Noel Browne, he of the way-ahead-of-its-time (but ultimately ill-fated) Mother and Child initiative in 1950. Browne, a medical doctor himself, was a survivor of T.B., which was then rampant in Ireland. He had seen both of his parents and most of his siblings die from T.B., and he was utterly passionate about eradicating this disease. Though he had absolutely no experience of politics, he joined *Clann na Poblachta*, successfully stood in the 1948 general election, and on his first day in *Dáil Éireann* he was surprisingly appointed Minister for Health. Undaunted, he set about his task with zeal. His lack of political experience was probably a huge benefit, because he refused to acknowledge the obstacles which other (supposedly wiser) colleagues pointed out to him. He introduced free screening for T.B. and, using the income and investments of the Hospital Sweepstakes, he built hospitals and sanatoria all over the country. And, to complete the equation, he began a search for the best possible medical staff available.

In particular, Browne decided that the country needed a Cardio Thoracic Surgeon and persuaded Dublin Corporation to advertise accordingly. Such advertisements were rare at that time, and luckily Maurice Hickey, still in London, became aware of it and applied for the position. Browne recognised him as the right man, in the right place, at the right time. The two men formed an immediate bond, and Browne gave his department officials the unequivocal instruction to "give Mr. Hickey whatever he wants."

And, while these momentous events were taking place in Dublin, there was I, bouncing, quite bold, but apparently healthy two-year-old in Cork, oblivious—as were my Ma and Da—of the fact that I had a very serious genetic heart disorder, i.e. a seriously large hole in my heart.

The (now defunct) Health Board structure wasn't introduced in Ireland until 1970, and back in the late 1940s and early 1950s it was the local authorities, city and county councils, who were responsible for managing the health system. And Maurice Hickey, the country's first local authority Cardio Thoracic Surgeon, was a busy man. Theoretically appointed by Dublin Corporation, he was in fact responsible for the entire country. New thoracic surgery theatres were opened in Rialto in Dublin, in Mallow in Co. Cork, and in Castlerea in Co. Roscommon and, driving his wife's car, he travelled to these locations on a rotating basis, performing operations in Rialto on Tuesdays, Mallow on Wednesdays, Castlerea on Thursdays, and back to Dublin on Fridays. Maurice Hickey himself later said that he realised the huge task facing him, as thoracic surgeons were a very rare commodity, and he knew that, when not in operating theatres, he would be travelling the roads of Ireland day and night. Such was the shortage of funding, he brought his own instruments with him and when Browne and his department offered him a chauffeur-driven car, he refused point blank.

"It would be a waste of public money," he said. "The chauffeur would have nothing to do for hours on end while I'm operating."

And so, in his first year, driving himself between the three locations, Maurice Hickey carried out 265 major operations.

In addition to his actual surgical work, the management of three surgical units, and a heavy administrative workload, he also kept up with all the latest international surgical developments and techniques. Meantime, his own work set new standards. In 1949 he became the first surgeon in Ireland to successfully operate on blocked mitral heart valves and, during the early 1950s, he became particularly interested in congenital heart disease. Based on his tireless and pioneering work, two further surgeons were appointed, one in Dublin and one in Galway, and this allowed Maurice Hickey to move south on a full-time basis. He continued to work in the Mallow Chest Hospital and also in St. Finbarr's Hospital, Cork. Then, in 1956, he relocated to the new St. Stephen's Hospital which had just opened at Sarsfield's Court, near Glanmire in Co. Cork.

That same year, a cardiologist by the name of Raymond Shanahan returned to Cork, having spent a year as the Ainsworth Scholar in Massachusetts General Hospital, Boston. Though he had accepted the post of Registrar at St. Finbarr's Hospital, Maurice Hickey encouraged Shanahan to join him at St. Stephen's Hospital, which in time became locally known simply as "Sarsfield's Court." There, they continued to introduce new procedures such as cardiac catheterisation and pacing and, in addition to being a T.B. hospital, Sarsfield's Court now became a centre for heart surgery with excellent results in the areas of closing patent ductus arteriosus, closed mitral valvotomy and pulmonary valvotomy. In 1960, another important addition to the team was anaesthetist Des Gaffney and, combining animal laboratory research with their clinical work, the three men continued to pursue their goal of achieving the highest world standards. Together, funded by World Health Organisation scholarships, they visited centres in the U.S., Scandinavia, and the U.K. Maurice Hickey's interest in congenital heart disease had never waned and subsequent developments, in the early 1960s, allowed surgery with profound hypothermia for coarctation of the aorta and septal defects.

And so, Maurice Hickey and his team began to carry out the first surgery in Ireland to repair septal defects, i.e. holes in peoples' hearts. They completed a number of successful operations on babies and young children but, in other cases, their results were hampered by haemolysis with profound bleeding.

This, then, is where I come into the story. For years, my parents and I had known that I had a heart murmur. This was attributed to a diagnosis of rheumatic fever when I was seven years old, though whether I ever actually had this condition or not remains a moot point. The first time I heard it, I thought the doctor said, "room attic fever." Which made no sense at all to me. But one way or another, the existence of this "murmur" meant that I was under strict orders during my young life not to overdo it, and to avoid anything that would cause undue perspiration. I was supposedly banned from most forms of activity that came naturally to an active child or to an energetic teenager. I say "supposedly" because, to my now shame, I blithely ignored these instructions and engaged in anything and everything, mostly behind my parents' backs. For example, having managed to acquire a pair(?) of different sized football boots, I persuaded a pal to keep them in his parents' shed. Despite my precautions, I was often caught and "murdered" for being in a bog of sweat, but in my mind the sheer enjoyment of running, playing sport, or whatever, was well worth whatever punishment might ensue. To be fair, as I never once showed any ill-effects from my exertions, the rules became more relaxed with the progression of my teenage years, and Ma and Da began to accept that perhaps I could "overdo it" from time to time. This meant I could play more sport, I could run, get sweaty, and even join the *Fórsa Cosanta Áitiúil* (a reserve army unit) which involved quite vigorous activities. And there were still no visible problems of any kind, so by the time I left school in 1964 I was to all intents and purposes a normal, active, healthy eighteen-year-old.

Having done well in my Leaving Cert exams, I was lucky enough to have a choice of jobs, of which joining a small local bank was the most appealing. Now part of a large financial organisation and still struggling to recover from the 2008 financial crisis, in 1964 this little bank was a small non-profit savings institution, albeit with great plans for the future. I began work in early September, and a week later the manager's secretary informed me that I had to go for my medical. This was so routine at the time that new employees could commence work before it was completed. I was told to head down to a Dr. Jerry Murphy on South Mall, that it wouldn't take long, and that I'd be back at work soon. Which I was. Dr. Jerry Murphy struck me as a kindly, old, possibly semi-retired doctor, who weighed me, took measurements, checked blood pressure, looked into mouth, eyes, and ears and, with his stethoscope, listened to my heart and lungs. No problem.

It came as a surprise therefore when, a few days later, the manager's secretary told me that I was to go for another medical, this time to a different doctor. This other doctor, based on St. Patrick's Hill, was none other than consultant cardiologist, Mr. Raymond Shanahan. To his eternal credit, Dr. Murphy had detected something in my heartbeat, something more than a possible post room-attic-fever murmur, and Mr. Shanahan (who took an E.C.G. reading and sent me for a chest X-ray) was soon to drop a bombshell. Back then, anybody aged under twenty-one was still considered to be a minor so, not being allowed to tell me anything directly, he requested that Ma and Da would call to see him.

It was Da therefore who sat me down in the front bedroom for the serious chat. The bottom line was that I had been born with a very large hole in my heart and that, unless it was repaired, I would be dead within a few years. The prognosis, quite simply, was that I was unlikely to show any symptoms until one day when I would collapse, turn blue, and die. Surgery was the only option, and the sooner the better. There was no other treatment. I remember that conversation with Da quite well. Strangely enough, though I did realise the seriousness of the situation, I wasn't particularly scared or nervous.

The next step was for the three of us (Ma, Da and me) to meet Mr. Shanahan again. He had a quiet authority, he was extremely professional and very matter-of-fact. It was clear that surgery was absolutely necessary. He did not hide the severity of the operation, or the serious risks involved, including the fact that I "might not come through it." However, he also told us that I was an extremely fortunate young man, as one of the top heart surgeons was just down the road, and that he had agreed to take me as a patient. A man by the name of Mr. Maurice Hickey.

The much later obituary in *The Irish Times* includes a description of Maurice Hickey as

> "A larger-than-life figure, well over 6 ft., carefully groomed, broad-shouldered, with trademark centre parting of his huge head of hair. Nothing but the best was good enough for his patients. He was dogmatic, ruthless, not particularly popular with colleagues, and often rubbed people up the wrong way."

This, in my opinion, is an excellent and accurate description. And I would add, as a patient of his, that it was abundantly clear that he took great care and had a deep personal interest, not only in the mechanics of the delicate and extremely tricky surgery required, but also in his patient as an individual human being.

St. Stephen's Hospital in Sarsfield's Court was a bare eight years old when I was admitted in October 1964. I had never previously been in hospital, so this was a new experience. A brand new dressing gown was bought for me, made of "pure Foxford wool," I think it cost £4.15s.0d., and (madness indeed) it still hangs in my wardrobe today.

My initial reaction was that the hospital was large, bright, but very clinical. The cardiac ward was on the third floor. Almost all of the rooms there were private, for individual patients. There was a lot of terrazzo on the floor and the predominant colours were green and beige. On exiting the lift, one turned right onto a long corridor, and all of the rooms were on the left-hand side. Each room had a bed, a locker, two chairs, a wardrobe, and a sink. Each room also had a balcony, and a view over the countryside. After all, it was designed and constructed as a T.B. hospital, and access to clean, clear air was important.

Having been admitted, the early part of my stay was taken up with E.C.G.s, X-rays, and a variety of other tests. I wasn't "sick," so for the rest of this time I was reasonably free to walk the corridor, chat to the nurses, etc. I also learned a lot about the other patients, all of them male, there being a separate corridor on another floor for females. The majority were much older than me. Many were quite ill and were either recovering from, or waiting for, surgery. From my first day there, I would see patients being trundled off to the operating theatre on their gurneys or—more scarily—seeing them returning later, complete with drips, tubes, oxygen tanks, etc. Soon after I arrived, a red-faced farmer from Co. Tipperary was admitted. He had huge hands, a tweed sportscoat, and a brand new suitcase. I never knew his name but when I met him in the corridor another patient was being wheeled back from the theatre, with all sorts of bottles and tubes and worried-looking nurses and a smell of Jeyes Fluid. The following day the farmer was nowhere to be seen. Later I overheard one of the nurses saying that he had absconded during the night.

I particularly remember a young lad by the name of Steve who was fifteen years old and also waiting for surgery. He was from Lahinch, Co. Clare, and I remember thinking how fortunate I was to be so close to home as I had a regular stream of visitors. Steve was lucky to have one a week. He was a grand youngfella and we used to chat about sport, hurling, English soccer, and whatever news might be on the newspaper. We also played cards. Just for fun.

Sometimes if things weren't too busy one or two of the nurses might join us for a hand of cards. I knew quite a few of them by name, unusual enough in those days when they were all called "sister." There was one young nurse on whom I had a huge crush. Secretly, of course. But she was about twenty-four or twenty-five, a huge age gap then compared to a raw eighteen-year-old. Kathleen Ryle, a lovely Kerry girl, from somewhere near Tralee. My aunts, and indeed neighbours, especially Mrs. O'Sullivan, unwittingly fuelled my crush by sending a seemingly endless supply of home-baked cakes and creamy buns to me. I'm not sure if they thought I was in the trenches or what, but they were extremely thoughtful. Of course, there was no way, even with Steve's help, that I could keep up with the supply, and so the surplus found its way to the nurses' room across the corridor. The prime time for consumption of these goodies was about 10 p.m. By then, those on night shift had completed their rounds, dispensed the medication, felt the pulses, checked the temperatures, and most of the inmates were settled for the night. Except yours truly who, being (a) eighteen, (b) not sick," and (c) the supplier of the cakes, was welcome to join the bun feast. And as luck would have it, Kathleen Ryle was often on night duty. Dream on, boy, dream on.

I had a regular stream of visitors. Family, relatives, friends, neighbours, the odd former classmate, and work colleagues. All very welcome. On one occasion though, a Wednesday afternoon (half-day at the bank), a group of colleagues arrived en bloc. Perhaps six or seven of them, they all crowded into my room and before long the craic was mighty. Laughing and joking. And smoking. Yes, in those days there was no such thing as a smoking ban and hospital visitors were allowed to smoke. The day was damp and chilly, the windows were closed, and soon the air was blue with cigarette smoke. Then in walked Mr. Hickey. He absolutely abhorred smoking. With a passion. After all, he had seen hundreds if not thousands of diseased and ruined lungs, and damaged hearts and arteries. He cleared the room faster than Jesus hunted the traders and the money lenders out of the temple. Then he gave me (another) severe lecture about the dangers of smoking, actively or passively, which I am ashamed to say took me many years to heed. My colleagues were still outside in the corridor, and I don't know what sort of a look Maurice Hickey gave them but, after he left, they came in sheepishly, singly or in twos, to bid me farewell and good luck.

I invented other ways to pass the time. Having a set of playing cards, I knew at least three types of patience or solitaire, and I made up other games. I had magazines and books and read whatever I had. On one occasion, I got *The Cork Examiner*, started at the top left-hand corner of the front page, and read every single word, in order, including all of the classified ads, planning notices, etc. down to the last word at the bottom right-hand corner of the back page. Should I be embarrassed to say that I made a list of my visitors, giving those who came more than once an extra tick for each visit? And I had a transistor radio— however, in those days, I could only get Radio *Éireann* (a single channel), which only broadcasted at certain hours, and anyway the reception in Sarsfield's Court was very crackly at times. Then, just when it seemed everything was A-OK for surgery, a problem arose. My operation required an ongoing blood transfusion. I learned that, before World War II, transfusions were only possibly when the donor(s) attended the hospital where the patient was, and the blood was directly transfused during the operation from donor to patient. The Irish Blood Transfusion Service Board did not come into existence until 1965, but Noel Browne as Minister for Health had established a National Blood Transfusion Association in 1948 (God bless him).

Blood however was a scarce enough commodity in 1964, and in my case the problem was greatly exacerbated with the discovery that I was O Negative, one of the rare blood groups and also, of the eight types, the only one that can only receive blood from donors with the same blood type. Thus, the hospital had to ensure that they would have a sufficient supply of my blood type and, as it was going to take some time to secure this, I was told I could go home in the interim.

Not only was blood in short supply, it was also very expensive, and Da was facing a substantial bill for this. Luckily, there was an option open to him, which nowadays seems strange, to say the least. If Da could round up a minimum of thirty donors, each donating a pint of their blood (irrespective of type), in my name, before a certain date, then the blood for my transfusion would be free. Da began the campaign, the result being that the number of donors greatly exceeded what was required, with all of the workers and staff of Cork Harbour Commissioners (where Da worked) answering the call.

By mid-November I was back in Sarsfield's Court. The date for surgery was set for Tuesday, November 17. My Da's birthday. Both Ma and Da were extremely worried, as were all the immediate and extended family, friends, and neighbours. Oddly enough, I was still quite calm. By now I was well used to E.C.G.s, heart, lungs, and chest X-rays and the like. Mr. Hickey looked in at least once every day, but usually it was more often. When accompanied by his large retinue of junior doctors, interns, matrons, staff nurses, junior nurses, and Uncle Tom Cobley and all, he could be gruff and abrupt, but he was always far more personal when he dropped in on his own, usually in late afternoon or early evening after surgery was finished for the day. He was the essence of professionalism. He exuded confidence.

On the eve of the operation, I had two interesting callers.

The first was a doctor, a member of the surgical team, who came to explain what was going to happen the next day, and to answer any questions. This approach was quite unusual at that time. Though to be honest, while I had no thoughts of absconding like the Tipperary man, I didn't want to know too many gory details either. As far as I was concerned, I was going to have surgery, recover, and be home for Christmas. Also, Mick Jagger and The Rolling Stones (then as big, if not bigger, than The Beatles) were due to play a concert in the Savoy on January 5, and I was expecting to be there.

At about 9 p.m., my second caller was the hospital chaplain, who came to give me Extreme Unction. This did give me some pause for thought as back in 1964 this was not the Sacrament of the Sick as it is known today—rather, it was very much the Sacrament of the Dying, administered only in the most serious situations. When the priest was finishd, he, too, asked if I had any questions and burst out laughing when I (quite innocently) enquired if it would be OK for me to go to the nurses' room to chat with them during their 10 p.m. tea-break. He told me that it was the first time in his life that he had administered Extreme Unction to someone who then wanted to get out of the bed to go and have a chat with people. And by the way, he told me he could see no reason why not.

I have absolutely no memory of the operation itself. I only know what I was subsequently told. There was an international audience—surgeons and other professionals who had come to observe a technique which had not previously been used in Ireland. Up to then, the procedure for open-heart surgery was to make a long, curved incision around the side and back of the patient and to gain access to the heart that way. In my case, Mr. Hickey made a much smaller incision down the centre of my chest, broke the breastbone, and opened the ribcage like a pair of double gates, thus achieving direct access to my heart. While I had known that this would be the approach used, I was unaware that it was new in this country.

The surgery itself lasted for seven hours. It was long and complicated. I recall waking up in intensive care, but this is a fleeting memory.

Because it seems that I crashed and was rushed back to theatre. I had stopped breathing. In order to get my lungs pumping again, Mr. Hickey and his team performed an emergency tracheotomy. They made an incision in my throat (scar still visible after fifty-several years) and inserted a tube into my windpipe, which in turn was attached to a heart-lung machine which worked an electric pump to make my lungs inflate and deflate so that I was "breathing," albeit by artificial means. I'm sure that there are far better explanations available as to how this works.

While this was going on, I experienced a very definite out of body experience. From quite a height, certainly much higher than any ceiling, I remember looking down on the surgical team frantically working on me. This wasn't frightening, it didn't last long, it may or may not have been a near death experience, but it remains vividly fixed in my memory.

Though I came off the heart-lung machine within a day or so, I remained in a critical condition, lapsing in and out of consciousness for the rest of that week. Everybody was dreadfully worried that I wouldn't come through. Some years later, my aunt told me that Da, who had to sign the surgery consent form because I was technically a minor, expressed the fear that he had signed my death warrant.

Two things about this period come to mind.

The quietest room in the cardiac ward was the last on the left at the very end of the corridor, and the most critically ill patients were moved into this room. I was aware that the man in this room had died on Wednesday night; another very sick patient was moved in on Thursday, and he too died there; on Friday his place was taken by an older patient, who died there early on Saturday morning. One, two, three, all gone. I was moved in there on Saturday evening. I wasn't given any explanation but I remember thinking, "Nope, this ain't going to happen," and, if anything, this move strengthened my resolve to recover.

The other thing was that at one stage I woke up and demanded to see Mr. Hickey. I had no idea what day it was, or what time of day, but I was later told that it was late evening on a Friday. Mr. Hickey of course was not in the hospital, and the nurses asked why I wanted to see him, but I refused to tell them, or indeed to tell any member of staff. Apparently, I just kept asking to speak to Mr. Hickey, but then I'd zonk out again. Lo and behold, he turned up. Later I learned that it was two o'clock in the morning they woke me and there he was, standing at my bedside, wearing a dress suit. No, it wasn't a dream. His wife, attired in evening gown, stood by his side. They had been attending some formal dinner, or maybe a ball, but the hospital staff had instructions to contact him any time if they thought it necessary. This was typical of the man. It was also long, long before mobile phones or suchlike, but they tracked him down at a hotel and, having received the message, he immediately decided to drive to Sarsfield's Court, along with dress suit, Mrs. Hickey, and all.

My question? What was it I wanted to know, what was so important that I would only accept an answer from the man himself?

"If I ever get married, and have children, could this hole-in-the-heart problem be hereditary?"

"No," he answered. Just a simple "No," and with that he introduced me to his wife (who was charming), they both shook hands with me, and they left.

By early the following week, I was on the road to recovery, but still very weak. Unable to even sit up on my own, I had to use a cut length of sheet which was tied to the end of the bed. This was knotted along its length and so I could pull myself, hand over hand, into a sitting position. The nurse whose idea it was called it my "donkey" and, even if they were around, the nurses insisted that I do it myself. Handy thing, that donkey.

The tube in my windpipe stayed in for quite a while (just in case), although they literally put a cork in the opening. This meant that I could remove the stopper, or quickly pull it in and out, and could make amusing whistling noises. Quite daft. Of course, when the stopper was out, I couldn't speak, as the tracheotomy was below my larynx.

I started listening to my crackly radio again, as I had been told to tune in to Hospital Requests. My Auntie May had written in requesting something by Elvis. Yes, my name and Get Well request were included, but the song played was "Walk Tall" by Val Doonican. Auntie May, I believe, had mixed feelings about this but I thought that the song title was quite apt.

One of the most difficult things was that I had to keep coughing on demand. Mr. Hickey would stride into the room unannounced, saying, "Cough, boy, cough," and would not leave until my cough was sufficiently strong to satisfy him. This was most uncomfortable and extremely sore, because of course my whole chest was very tender inside and outside, but the coughing had to be strong enough to clear fluid out of my lungs. My chest was protected, initially by some sort of plaster cast, subsequently in very heavy bandages. Then came the day when the bandages were removed. Mr. Hickey looked at me, told me that it wouldn't hurt, that they would be gentle, then he nodded to one of the senior nurses (she of the donkey idea—another lovely woman) who carefully took hold of the top of these bandages and then immediately ripped them off in one go. Gentle, how are you?

I will dwell no longer on the recovery process. Mr. Hickey, however, did inform me that the hole in my heart was "the size of an orange" and that, at that time, I was the oldest patient in Ireland to survive hole-in-the-heart repair surgery. Whether or which, I was home in time for Christmas and, yes, I did get to see The Rolling Stones early in January. And I was back working in the bank by early February—I was and am very grateful for the fact that, even though they had no obligation to do so, they kept my job open for me.

I still had to have regular check-ups with Mr. Hickey. Initially these were weekly, then fortnightly, monthly, and annually for perhaps two or three years. They took place in Sarsfield's Court, and Da used always insisted that he would drive me down. I understood why. Naturally, I had (still have) the highest respect for Mr. Hickey but, to the day he died, Da was in even greater awe of him than I ever was.

One Sunday morning in the late autumn of 1989 I strayed into Mass in St. Augustine's Church in Cork. The sermon was one of the shortest and most powerful I have ever heard. The basic message was to say "Thank you," and the priest challenged us to think of somebody to whom we owed something in our lives, and to go and say "Thank you."

The name of Mr. Maurice Desmond Hickey came to mind, and I wondered if I had ever thanked him properly? Retired at this stage, he lived in Douglas West (his house, "Clooney," has since been demolished to make room for apartments), and I decided that, yes, I should go tell him in person.

It was almost November by the time I got around to ringing him and I realised that twenty-five years had passed since he had saved my life. When I rang to make an appointment, the phone was answered by his housekeeper (a very competent lady). Explaining why, I arranged a visit for November 17. I asked Da if he would come with me. I knew he'd say yes.

"Are you the boy from twenty-five years ago?" the housekeeper asked, and as she showed us in, she whispered to me, "He's very pleased about that, you know."

Mr. Hickey was genuinely delighted to see both of us, we had tea and a lovely chat, and I was truly glad to have that opportunity to say 'Thank you' to him in person. The events of 1964 not only saved my life, they shaped it.

The slivers of fortune, why I chose to work for that small organisation, the sharp ear of Dr. Jerry Murphy as he listened through his stethoscope, the coincidence of time and place that allowed Noel Browne, Maurice Hickey and Raymond Shanahan to have so much in readiness—just for me, or so it seemed. But no, I realised, not just for me but for every patient, regardless of race, creed, colour, or station of life.

I saw and learned from the goodness of people, the strength of family, the kindness of strangers. Over those few months, I came to understand Ma and Da, the true nature of parenting, the formation of a new and wiser bond, never to be broken.

Many actors were involved, some played leading roles, others had bit parts, and all of them, whether they knew it or not, they were excellent teachers.

Maurice Hickey strode that stage like a colossus. Highly skilled, yes, but also professional, far-seeing, tireless, dedicated, passionate. Above all, he looked beyond the ailment, beyond the condition and, literally and metaphorically, he looked into and touched the heart of the individual. My continuing existence on this earth is testament to his ability, but his impact on my life has been profound.

Thank you, Maurice Desmond Hickey, you were indeed an extraordinary man.

John FitzGerald

The Island

We spared nowhere that day on The Gearagh,
your courage spurring me on to cross
the sunken stretch at the end of the old road
where we could explore the undulating

woodland I had admired so often
from a distance—to discover its hillocks were
just builders' rubble from another time
when that kind of thing was permissible;

and across the mudflats I was always told
would swallow a man whole
I followed your lead, as you would gauge
the hidden depth of step perfectly,

thrilling in the sinking in and hauling out
again; until we reached the island
I had never thought I would find a way
to get to, going into the thicket centre

and calling for you to follow me.
But you just stood out there, waiting,
all light draining into the darkening mire,
as if to say: you go on, I will stay

apart now out here, while I have no need.

James McKeon

The Promise

It was Christmas Eve. There was a light fall of snow as my Uncle Paddy paid the taxi driver and eased his tired legs out of the cab. He smiled when he noticed the silver road sign on the wall of the little corner shop—SUN VALLEY DRIVE; how life had changed; California here we come. It had been plain Well Lane when he'd last been here over fifty years ago. Pat never married. He had a long relationship with Arthur Guinness. He paused to get his bearings. He felt lost, surrounded by ghosts, and wondered if progress was really going backwards as he struggled across the road in the stiff breeze and made his way along what had once been the playground of his youth. Well Lane was long gone, and the vast North Link Highway swept off into the horizon.

Pat was born at home on the 7th June 1942. While war raged in Europe life in Ireland freewheeled along in blissful neutrality. Someone said it was one of the rare times the Irish refused a fight. He was a chubby little boy with a mop of curls and a face plastered with freckles. Women admired his curls. Pat hated them. But every time he sneaked into his mother's room, borrowed her scissors, and cut one off, two seemed to grow. Although surrounded by a large family he always seemed to be alone reading a book, fascinated by men conquering mountains or brave explorers on a treacherous mission to the North Pole. His early life was overflowing with mythical heroes. Already a daydreaming child, these books fanned the flames of his vivid imagination.

The memories flooded back; the nonstop noise in the lane; dogs, cats, pigeons, children, the happiness in his old home with the grandiose name, Paddock House. The memories tumbled on, each one triggered off another. In his mind's eye he could see his mother waving her wooden spoon in the air like a musical conductor over her orchestra of children, a mother hen, boss in her own kitchen; "Fastest man gets the most"; "Your eyes are bigger than your belly." And his father dancing around the table, dodging and ducking, a crackling radio in his hand, listening to Joe Louis and Rocky Marciano fighting in Madison Square Garden. He was throwing punches and commentating, with a Woodbine clung to his lower lip, bobbing up and ducking down as he spoke. In reality Paddock House was an ivy-covered ramshackle old house surrounded by a neglected acre of nettles and stones. It was over a hundred years old with an open fire always heaped high with logs. There was one other room downstairs. Although seriously damp it had a hint of musty grandeur dominated by a large table with a torn ping-pong net attached to it, and an arrogant chandelier looking down on a worn carpet. A battered piano groaned apologetically in the corner. Dozens of sheet music of Irish melodies, covered with cobwebs, were stacked behind it; a spider's playground gathering dust. Outside, at the back of the house, stood a dilapidated toilet covered by sheets of corrugated tin. The inside toilet was a bucket on the upstairs landing.

A cloud of sadness hung over Pat as he sat on a bench in deep thought, surrounded by nothing. The quietness was interrupted by an occasional passing truck. Paddock House and this whole area had been an idyllic upbringing for an impressionable young boy: a jungle filled with mystery, oceans of muck as a playground, gooseberry bushes, two chickens, an old donkey named Napoleon and an Aladdin's cave of unexplored sheds. The undergrowth was teeming with rabbits, an occasional fox, and a lurking hawk could be seen circling the skies above ready to swoop. When his parents were out, he sometimes struggled onto Napoleon's back. It was difficult with his bony-sparrowed legs but some days he got carried away in his own fantasy world, saving damsels in distress and shooting imaginary Indians with an imaginary gun while dodging imaginary arrows. They were innocent times, yet a cruel savagery lurked in the background which was deemed to be the norm. A captured cat would be callously thrown to a pack of dogs and cheered while it was torn to shreds; old dogs would be regularly hung from nearby trees, and it wasn't confined to animals; a handicapped boy, about Pat's own age, convulsed in a fit, would continually bash his head against a wall until the frenzy subsided or he knocked himself unconscious. It frightened him to see the boy lying on the ground, froth on his mouth, his face covered in blood, at peace with the world, until the next fit. It also showed the cruelty of that time when it was common, and accepted, to see a sealed bag of unwanted pups dumped in the stream. Yet, all through the summer, this innocuous stream was their Riviera, their Nirvana. In their ignorance these boys knew nothing else. The stream was banked up with rocks and sods, and this was where he learned to swim. He didn't care about pollution, dead dogs, water rats or broken bottles.

As he sat there engulfed in the deafening silence it was difficult to imagine the way it once was. It was as if being poor had been a common bond. Lady Poverty ruled with an empty fist and never seemed to lower her ugly head. His strongest memory growing up was utter poverty. This was the main reason why he was forced to emigrate; get out or perish, be sucked up into a never-ending web of apathy; the Big Apple or bust. All through his young days he survived on a few pence by delivering bags of turf in a box-cart to neighbours in the lane. The bags were bigger than himself and they were hosed down by the shady turf dealer to make them heavier.

The falling snow reminded him that there was one special time of the year when everyone forgot their troubles. Christmas was bewitching; the innocent expectation of Santa's arrival, the presents, nothing was expected, anything was welcome, He smiled at the memory; a flash-lamp with no batteries; a cap gun which was grand until the caps ran out; visiting church cribs and comparing them. It always seemed to be snowing. He knew Christmas had arrived when the tree appeared in the front room. This was his father's job and he always made Pat feel special by asking him to help. It was nothing elaborate; just a plain tree he had chopped down, stuck in a bucket of sand and plonked in the corner but, to the children, it was magical. Then the big red candle was placed in the window and lit by the youngest in the family.

Pat felt a sense of wonder as he walked up the narrow, bockety, red-bricked Well Lane with each window overflowing with colour, glittering in the blackness of the night.

As a boy he was fascinated by Tom Murphy, the local blacksmith who worked behind the quarry. Tom was a broad-shouldered man with a black face and a club foot. Pat loved to linger in the background and watch him, drenched in sweat, eyes flashing with satisfaction, lost in his work; the hiss of the sizzling steam when the steel shoe was placed in the water; the rhythmic beat of the hammer striking the anvil as he shaped the shoe to fit the hoof; the pungent smell while the red-hot shoe was being nailed on to the burning hoof.

Back then religion had played a major part in everyone's life. The priest was God. When the feast of Corpus Christi came along the local women would get buckets of water from the old well and religiously scrub down every inch of Well Lane on their hands and knees in preparation for the passing procession. One day a girl in the lane got married. As she walked to the church, all dressed in white, she stopped at her friend's house on the corner, borrowed her wedding ring, and carried on down the hill to the church for the ceremony. Like the pied piper of Hamlin, a flock of inquisitive children, including Pat, trailed in her wake to the church gates. She got married, walked back with her husband, returned the ring to her friend, and had a knees-up in her little house. Pat smiled at the memory. They were such practical times.

The cinema had played a huge part in their young lives. His father gave him six pence every Friday night. The Plaza was his Mecca, the centre of his life. In reality it was a glorified flea pit; three pence to get in but a jam jar was also accepted as payment. Glass was scarce in post-war Ireland and the local jam factory paid the cinema three pence for each jar. That little cinema was noisy. It was rough. It was filthy but to them it was a magnetic wonderland. They were bewitched, transported to the American Wild West, the jungles of darkest Africa or to the far-off North Pole. With their hearts in their mouths they could witness Tarzan wrestling with a deadly crocodile, the crocodile didn't stand a chance, the Durango Kid or Hopalong Cassidy single-handedly out-shoot a tribe of Cherokee Indians, or Captain Marvel and Flash Gordon take on the evil Emperor Ming as he tried to take over the galaxy. They lived every second of those films with an animated passion, cheering if the hero won, warning him if he was in any danger and booing at the nasty villain. For years those boys lived for Friday nights. Pat's six pence wages stretched a long way; after the cinema it was two pence for a bag of chips and, finally, six rock-like toffees for the last penny.

He shivered as he sat on the bench alone. He was running out of memories. There were ghosts everywhere. He gazed across SUN VALLEY DRIVE at the empty concrete playground. The Well Lane boxing club once stood there until one night it was blown away in a storm. Next to that was the little convent dancehall run by the nuns. He had been desperately shy but one night he took the plunge. He borrowed his big brother's old suit from the wardrobe and trimmed his curls until the mirror told him he looked alright. Then he soaked himself with innocent eau-de-Cologne. Pat felt all dolled up and ready for action but there was no chance of any hanky-panky. The convent insisted that all couples had to stay one foot apart. Lurking in the background was a frightening deterrent; a posse of passionate nuns, each one, like hawk-eye, armed with a twelve-inch ruler. They were determined that the sweating bodies remained one foot apart. Then at nine o'clock everyone threw themselves down on their knees and recited a decade of the Rosary led by the nuns. Looking back he smiled at the pain of his first real dance. Every time he asked a girl to dance that night she refused him. It was one excuse after another. One girl said, "No, I'm sweating. Ask my sister."

After all those years it still hurt and, that night, as he walked home alone the stars shivered in the black sky. They seemed to wink and mock him. Later he lay in bed, frail and vulnerable, his head filled with lonesome thoughts, until the tears came and sent him to sleep.

Pat sighed. He had seen enough. He'd kept his promise; one last look. The hustle and bustle and laughter of Well Lane were no more; flattened by bureaucratic bulldozers. He felt sad. It was time to go. He took a crumpled letter from his pocket. It was an appointment with his doctor in Manhattan. The cancer was back. He crumpled the letter in a ball and threw it in a bin by the corner. The snow stopped. He smiled and walked down the hill.

Bill O'Connell

Solo

Music infuses our primitive stem,
imbues the muscle
with its charge. When we die, light
dissipates, rises into air.
Hiking last month.
I went down a trail at dusk.
A coyote called and I stopped,
started again. Again the animal's voice
struck through the trees, my chest.
Later, listening to Miles Davis,
I sensed in his trumpet that same fierce
beckoning breaking through
our resistance. The audience
unwilling to let him
go, wanting it again,
over and over, that cry.

I Asked Her to Sing the Oldest Song She Knew

Nadia was trying to tell me
about her sailor boyfriend:
"Yorktown" she said
in thick Russian, waving
her hands as she spoke, "his ship."
She made a boat out of paper,
folding it up in the weak, midnight
light of Pskov through the dirty
sixth floor window,
her hands making their own shapes
as she folded, unfolded,
and began again.
Later, she sang in that tiny kitchen,
her hands strumming a homemade guitar.
She turned her voice to the window,
reaching into that ancient city
for the next line and the next.

Skipping Mass

I walked out of childhood, skipped Mass
and went to a pond in the woods, sure that
a streak of sun on a high boulder, on me,
was purer than the words of priests
who fidgeted with their vestments
and spoke of their mothers with tears.
The courage of listening to my own mind,
to break the rules and never confess again.

I didn't find God in the woods but birdsong,
sunlight, the favors of mid-morning, ivy
twisting around a sapling, reaching up, up.
We can't help but love the sky.
Each time faith appears, I fear it still:
a desire to be heard, but not known.

Bargaining (Easter Rites)
for Missy M. M.

God borrows our tongue.
Naming, the ancients said,
is in itself a false beginning.

God, you said, spoke to you thrice
while you were brushing your teeth.

Be mine in English, no accent.
Be mine. Be mine. A pronoun.

I am an infant at this,
rolling over, joyful feet kicking.

*

Something's out there and nearby,
not a bird but moving from tree to tree.
March and the earth opens up. Beasts

crawl out through the last bits
of crusty snow to read
the clear pattern of stars.

I used to believe they called to me,
full of my sin and sorrow,
looking to devour the rest.

At dawn, I stoke last night's fire.
No one comes for me but me.

*

Let me open my eyes.
No confessions: even to God
but I resist less and less.

Today on the path around
Ludlow Reservoir, I spoke
to the woods, the canopy, saying

take me, show me, but don't
touch me, don't inhabit me, don't
make me insane or always blissful.

Chainsaws in the distance.
Children next door: dusk.

*

When the wren sings, it's not joy.
Even if that is what we feel.
Its singing is not for us.

The wren sings to make more
wrens to sing. One note wavers
just enough out of tune

to make it new. We name it
because we must, because
God has no mouth.

When We Were All Still Alive

Back when everyone was alive
we'd sing around the piano:
my father, Mrs. Barry, McGurty—
cousins and neighbors standing three rows deep.
Someone to turn the page, to bring a drink
for the piano player, Mrs. Barry, and later, me,
when we were all still alive.

I keep a picture on my piano, all of us
singing Christmas carols, mouths open
and eyes lit up with red and green lights,
that big old gold mirror in the front room
reflecting all of us back to ourselves
when we were all still alive, singing.

I glance at it late at night when I play
for all of us then, "My Funny Valentine" and
"Dancing in the Dark," beyond the single lamp,
voices rushing in to fill
the silence between notes.

Luke

(1987-2006)

Luke is dead, my son's friend—
slipping off suddenly with
a stopped heart.
No one can explain it,
though rumor tries—
the whole senior class
at his wake. Now,
what remains? All of them
moving on, more serious, into
late summer. Today
at the funeral
the priest said
God did not pluck
Luke from this earth, but
loves him now. That he is
beside the Lord, waiting for us.
I wished that thought upon
those kids crying in their
best clothes, even as I
thought otherwise, watching
my son clench his teeth

as he prayed, close to Jesus,
close to Luke, speaking
to the congregation
of his love for his friend,
making me
want to believe again.

Aisling Twomey

Hometown Legacy

I was born in a house on a hill in the small city of Cork, a few miles inland of the Atlantic Ocean. It's the sort of place where nothing significant ever happens, with its winding roads, back alleys and broad accents. The River Lee bisects the city, dividing it into the rich south side and the less privileged north. I learned my beat in Cork and it will always be home.

In Irish, Cork is called Corcaigh, which means "marsh." It's been a settlement since the 6th century, when Saint Finbarr collected students and founded a church and monastery on a cliff above the Lee. In his honour, half of Cork is called Finbarr and the others carry it as a middle name. With the name comes a strange sense of humour, self-deprecating to the nth and loaded with colloquialism. The people of Cork proclaim to take history in their stride. The city is, they say, the real capital of Ireland: *Luimneach a bhí; Baile Átha Cliath atá, Corcaigh a bheidh.*

Near the end of the street where I grew up on the south side, there is a pedestrian footbridge. The footbridge and the road it leads to are poorly lit and badly maintained, with small amounts of local traffic but little else. The bridge hosts gangs of adults drinking and gangs of teenagers drinking. The walls are daubed with unimaginative graffiti, enveloped by grungy gang messaging: IRA. HEAPHY'S RATS. NICE BAZZER. It's completely normal to find the occasional used needle poking out from small piles of illegally dumped rubbish. Every town has a place like this, a forgotten hole in the local history.

For as long as I can remember, my mother has favoured avoiding this bridge, but it's a shortcut to the city centre so everyone ignores her warnings—including herself. She has always told me to avoid the bridge after dark.

"Don't cross the bridge at night!" she says to anyone departing the house after twilight, even if she knows they're not going that way. The bridge is the sort of place that lends itself easily to accidents and easier still to menace.

A small city could never hold in my wild spirit of adventure, born of too much reading and no shortage of daydreaming. The financial crisis hit Ireland hard; I lit on out as soon as I could but somehow often found myself returning to my mother's house and the warm fire that illuminates her sitting room.

It was a completely ordinary Friday in October when I met George. The ground was wet from the misting rain that had deluged the country, but the sky was clear and the air crisp and fresh; I could see stars twinkling overhead and my breath rose up before me in little puffs of early winter. It was cold and dark and despite my mother's endless warnings, I gave in to the temptation of the shortcut and walked up over the bridge.

The Romans never conquered Ireland (a point of immense regional pride), so the country saw its first true changes during the Viking and Norman invasions. Arguably for Cork, things went downhill from there. In the Middle Ages there were a couple of thousand people in the town and half of them died of plague when the Black Death swept in. Truthfully, Cork has something of a habit for getting into trouble—in 1491, my unfortunate kinsmen accidentally got caught up in the Wars of the Roses, when a pretender to the throne sought support for a plot to overthrow Henry VII. A former Mayor of Cork agreed and took some men to England; they were all executed. After this event, Cork was called the Rebel County, and it's not for nothing. My grandmother would say, "God loves a trier."

Years have passed, but I remember the bridge like it was yesterday. I remember the orange glow of the lone streetlamp reflected softly on the wet ground. I remember the swoosh of the cars driving along beneath me. I came from the darkness, and he didn't see me but I did see him. I remember taking in his too-long white shirt, sleeves rolled up the elbows, and his tattered Converse.

We were walking towards one another in the narrow space,

but instead of continuing past me, he stopped and turned to aside. Thinking that he was clearly unhinged and that I could still turn around and walk away, I watched him pull himself up onto the railing of the footbridge. For a split second I didn't understand what was going on.

He took a big breath and pitched forward, leaning out over the dual carriageway. They say that in these moments, the adrenaline rushes and fight or flight kicks in. It's a cliché to say that my heart burst to life but I swear I could hear it pumping in my ears. Realisation dawned. He was going to jump.

"Please don't," I said loudly. "Please don't do that."

He hadn't expected me and I interrupted him. He reached out and grabbed hold of the suspension wire— the only thing that stopped his fall to a terrible end. My legs were weak, and my mouth was dry. I swallowed a few times. My hands were suddenly freezing, and I was wide awake, blood buzzing in my veins. Fight or flight.

"Just walk on girl, nothin' to do with you," he said.

"Please. I can't leave you here, and I don't want to watch. Please. Please don't make me watch this." For a long time, he looked down at me from the heights, weighing his desperate desire against my plea.

"Stay there," he said. "Don't move." His accent was thick and flat, but his voice was small and young; he was only a child. I stayed put, watching his descent.

He started to look around, sliding his hand down the wire so he could begin to lower himself to his knees. The railing was wet and I longed to turn my face away so I couldn't see if he slipped, but I couldn't look away. As soon as his Converse touched the ground, I dropped my bag and stumbled the last few steps. The relief was consuming and I started crying before I reached him. I grabbed him, this child I didn't know, and held him close, letting him sob into my shoulder. We were both shaking.

"It's okay," I said, "It's okay. You're down now, it's gonna be okay." He separated from me and in the orange glow I saw his face for the first time. "How old are you? What's your name?" I asked.

Ireland was fully colonised by the English between 1540 and 1603 during the Plantations, and again with the arrival of one Oliver Cromwell in 1649. In Ireland we know Cromwell as a genocidal maniac, but the English seem to think he's absolutely fabulous, so I suppose it all depends on your viewpoint. In Ireland, Cromwell set about his task with relish. His deep antipathy for Catholicism was borne out when he banned the faith, offered bounties for priests, and executed the ones he found. Penal Laws meant that land belonging to Catholics was confiscated and no Catholic was permitted to live in a town.

His men sacked Wexford, killing thousands, and setting it alight; Cork fell quickly in the aftermath. In Drogheda, Cromwell gave no quarter, referring to his savagery as "a righteous judgement of God on these barbarous wretches". You get the impression he was both a zealot and not much fun; thousands of Irish were transported as indentured labourers. Cromwell's actions bought famine and plague, widespread dispossession, and disenfranchisement. My people lost everything; everything was taken from them by force.

"I'm seventeen. George Ryan." He was still crying, and his voice was thick, but I told him my name and gave him another hug.

"Why were you on the bridge? Where do you live? Can I bring you home?" I had no idea what I was doing, but I couldn't leave him there and I was grasping for anything that might help.

"Nah, home is up in Knocknaheeney girl, it's ages away. I just couldn't take it anymore."

"Couldn't take what?" I asked, "What's going on that's made you this sad?"

"I'm sick of being mocked. All those stupid fucking bullies, they're always at me."

"For what?"

"I'm gay like," he said, looking down at his shoes.

"I'm sorry," I said, "That's shit." I didn't know what else to say.

"They're supposed to be my friends like. They're all over there," he said, gesturing to the other side of the bridge. "I don't want to go back to them." I glanced across and could hear vague shouts and chatter, carried a little on the wind to where we stood.

"Okay," I said, "So what are you gonna do, go home?"

"Yeah, fuck this girl, I'm going home to sleep. I've had loads to drink." I already knew that; his eyes were hazy and his words were slurred.

"Who are you going home with?" I asked. "I don't think you should go alone when you're this upset."

"Ah no, it's fine. Julie's down the road there, I'll ring her and we'll go home together."

"Can you ring her now, while I'm here?" I asked him. I didn't quite believe him, but he nodded and took his phone out of his pocket and rang Julie. To his credit, she answered and when he started crying again she said she'd come back for him. He hung up the phone.

"Listen," I said, "You're very drunk and you might not remember this tomorrow, but I really need you to message me as soon as you're home, so take down my number. And promise you'll message."

"I will, I will," he said, "What's the number?"

I watched him enter it into the phone.

"George, I know this won't make much sense right now, but the bridge isn't the answer, yeah? I think some day you'll have friends who won't be shitty." I felt useless, running out these pointless platitudes as though I could solve this boy's problems with just a few words in the dark.

"Thanks girl," he said. He gave me one last hug and then he left, walking down the bridge toward Julie, who was waving at him from the road beyond.

In the mid 1800s, an *Gorta Mór* came. It means "The Great Hunger," a famine so severe that it changed Ireland irrevocably. Proximally, the famine was caused by a potato blight that passed through Europe in the 1840s—but ultimately, Ireland was at the time part of the United Kingdom. Decisions made in London meant that Ireland exported its production of food crops and livestock, creating a starvation gap in which one million people died. A further million emigrated, birthing Ireland's status as a country of migrants. The population of Ireland has never recovered. "It was a genocide," people will say, "and they killed us by the million."

I turned away and walked the rest of the bridge, past the revelling teenagers George had left when he'd decided to throw himself into the next world. They were laughing and joking, hooting to the moon and cackling. Booze ran freely and they seemed to be having the time of their lives— young, free and untroubled in the cold night air. Drunk and miles from home, they had no idea that one amongst them had attempted to take his life just yards away. Ignoring the urge to scream at them, I hurried onward to the safety of my mother's kitchen.

George was not my first brush with suicide. I was six when I came downstairs one morning to find my mother in tears, the result of her brother's suicide outside his home in the suburbs. Shortly before he died, he bought me a new Barbie. I still have the doll, somewhere.

I was thirteen when my brother's best friend hung himself. Thinking about my teenaged brother in a too-big suit, shouldering the coffin of a boy he'd traded cards with, is hard to bear. My brother doesn't speak of it.

When I was seventeen, a cousin of mine went missing. Our extended family climbed into cars to find him, driving out into the freezing wet December night as a local radio announcer gave a physical description of him every few minutes. Michael is twenty-eight, tall and thin with bushy eyebrows. Last seen driving a Nissan Sunny.

They found the car on the side of a road; the fumes were overpowering. At the funeral, his mother collapsed, while his father met each visitor with a handshake, accepted all apologies, and shed not one tear.

"Nobody took him by the hand and told him what to do," he said to me. "I won't take his choice away from him." What are you supposed to say to that? What does that even mean?

By the early 1900s, Ireland was agitating for Home Rule,

demanding limited freedom from the British. Though this nearly came to pass, the outbreak of World War I in 1914 meant that Home Rule was shelved. Irish soldiers enlisted to fight with the British and Cork's Volunteers joined the Royal Munster Fusiliers. My father taught me that they suffered casualties in Gallipoli, at the Somme and at Passchendaele—no small burden, for a tiny corner of a still-growing Empire.

Back home in Ireland, at Easter 1916, revolution came. Launched by Irish republicans seeking an end to British rule, the Easter Rising lasted six days. Members of *Óglaigh na hÉireann*, the Irish Citizen Army and women from *Cumann na mBan* seized key locations in Dublin and proclaimed an Irish Republic. In Cork, 1000 Volunteers mobilised but didn't fight (unusual, given my ancestors' general proclivity for attempting this sort of thing). The Rising ended in surrender, and its seven leaders were executed by the British. They also arrested 3500 people (many of whom hadn't participated) and sent 1800 to internment camps in Britain.

"Obviously," my history teacher told us, "the sense of resentment against the British increased considerably."

A close friend at university called me one New Year's Eve and said it was done for him. He'd had enough of all the stars in all the skies.

"I have to go girl" he said, "My head is fucked." We stayed on the phone for eight hours, watching the sun rise. Every time he told me he had to go, I told him I still had something to say and could he hang on a minute? And together, between the pair of us, we decided against him going, after all. Each New Year's Eve he messages, to say thanks. "Another year done girl," he writes, "More to come."

I went to guitar lessons every Friday evening after school with my teenaged best friend. We would walk from the school gates up the Douglas Road and into Brian's house. We'd say hello, practice our chords, learn new songs and head home. Brian was a kind and loving man, with a young daughter he clearly doted on.

"She just amazes me every day," he would say. More than a

decade later, in December, I was home in Ireland for Christmas, driving across the city. There was a documentary on the radio about a local musician who had died by suicide. It took me a few seconds to recognise how I knew this name. My guitar teacher was gone, another soul lost to the ether.

Suicide is a legacy that haunts my family. I've never been able to conceptualise the sense of pain in my parents' hearts; I'm not sure I could bear it. I can't take the sadness away for them and for a time, I had nightmares that my father too would disappear beneath the makeshift noose, the exhaust fumes or the brown plastic bottle of pills. Once, while drunk, he became upset at the losses incurred.

"Oh Jesus," he said, "I worry so much about all of you."

So please, believe me when I tell you that I took George at his word when he said he just couldn't take it anymore. Please believe me when I tell you that I walked in my mother's door that evening and called the Gardaí. The local garda station is perhaps two minutes from the footbridge; George and Julie could be walking past it as I called.

Though the people of Cork didn't fight in the Easter Rising, they rose to the occasion during the War of Independence that followed. In 1919, the MPs elected from Ireland refused to take their seats in Westminster and set up a rebel parliament in Dublin. The British government sent in the Black and Tans and the Auxiliaries, who set about making themselves notorious. Statues in Cork tell the stories of the dead. In March 1920, the Lord Mayor of Cork Thomas Mac Curtain was shot at his home in front of his wife. His successor Terence McSwiney was arrested in August that year and died on hunger strike in October. In December, the Black and Tans set the city alight; the Burning of Cork claimed 300 buildings— and the local people continued their revolt regardless. At the end of the Civil War, Ireland was partitioned into the Free State and the six counties that now make up Northern Ireland; a direct result of the original plantations, some 300 years before.

The local units in Cork refused to accept the new reality and established a Munster Republic. Given the history of Cork so far, it should come as no surprise to learn that the Republic didn't last long, and that Cork was overtaken by the Free State forces.

My city also holds the dubious honour of being the place where the head of Government, Michael Collins, was assassinated at Béal na mBlath in 1922. Collins was himself from Cork. Legend has it that he was advised against going there but insisted that "They won't shoot me in my own county." Perhaps Collins had been away from home too long.

Denis O Neill fired the fatal shot; ironically a former British Army soldier who had fought in World War I, he knew Collins personally and had met him several times. Post mortem, Collins' men had to transport him 20 miles back the road to Cork City. The roads were blocked and the convoy travelled across fields and farms in the dead of night, sometimes carrying his corpse on their shoulders. They found Collins' diary in his pocket. His last words: "The people are splendid."

The sergeant in the public office heard my tale and told me that I would be better to call back later because this was 'a Monday morning type of issue' and the police were busy right now because the pubs and clubs were heaving.

"Can't you look for him?" I asked.

"Unfortunately not. Look, you did what you could, and he's gone home. He'll be fine."

When I got off the phone, I had no idea where to turn to or who to speak with. All I had was this kid's name and no weaponry to go to bat for him. I got a message about an hour later. "Hi dis is Julie. Georg is hme now tks grl." I never heard from either of them again.

After weeks of my chasing, the Gardaí finally called me to a meeting. They had found him, they said, at my insistence, and though he didn't remember my name, he recalled the bridge and the girl who got him off it. He was getting help, they said, for his drinking. He seemed fine; his mother and grandmother loved and supported him. He would be well.

But I couldn't forget George Ryan.

In the 1930s, the municipal government in Cork cleared the tenements of the inner city, and housing estates sprung up on the periphery of the town, mostly on the north side— the side where George came from, and my own father before him. And in the peacetime that followed the centuries of war and devastation, Cork thrived for a time—aside from the scourge of TB which ravaged the country in the 1930s and 40s, killing tens of thousands each year— and later the polio epidemic of 1956, which led to hundreds of children being evacuated out of the city to the countryside, among them my uncle.

In the years since I met George, I moved to Dublin and then to London. I changed career and fell in love with a man I met at an airport. I travelled the world. I sat with one of my best friends as she passed away in a hospital bed and I rang in every year with a promise that I would live a life of love, not limits.

Every now and then, I would check in on George's Facebook page, just to see how he was doing, to make sure he was okay and still cracking on with this living thing. I often thought about sending him a message, but I stopped myself each time. I felt I would be interfering.

A generation before my time and George's, Cork survived as a manufacturing town, with Ford, Dunlops and Verolme playing a big role in local employment. When they closed one after another in the early 1980s, Cork was devastated by unemployment. Woolworths left Ireland and closed their Cork store in 1984. Local offices were boarded up. Shops closed. Thousands of people were laid off and the bottom fell out of the world for many local families. People panicked. My parents tell stories of poverty and hunger. When they were George's age, Cork was on its knees. Perhaps the city was saved by the self-deprecating humour of Corkonians— but it was helped by the arrival of an almost unknown tech company which set up in Hollyhill on the north side; Apple employs six thousand people in Cork today.

George died in September, two years after I met him. I found out in December when I did my little check in, expecting to see his smiling happy face. There were thousands of messages from his friends and loved ones, covering over the ones that had pushed him to the grave. QUEER. FAG. FUCKING HOMO.

The footbridge is still there. And every time I am home, I cross it. I glance down there at night. I peer across it in the morning fog. I actively seek it out. It's the sort of place that can change lives, in a town where nothing significant ever happens.

Emily Rios

The River

I am this river and I have the last name to prove it. The length of the Merrimack River runs through Lowell and cuts the Centralville neighborhood from its city. My last name runs wild through each canal and dammed waterway. At first it bubbled with resentment. The red steel that rusted into a dried-blood coating nauseated me each time I crossed the "Achin"—Aiken-Street bridge. The emerald bridge a mile away seemed grander, happier, more alive. Each footstep would accentuate each bitter observation. The subsequent removal of our neighborhood sign from Achin's intersection made the water underneath boil and steam.

Yet, growing up alongside this gouge in the earth, paired with the intense rush of "not-earth," lit a spark of imagination that burned uncontrollably. I observed the variability of the world through its consistency in the Merrimack. I cannot imagine not living beside these currents, though if I did, the world would be an uninspired mound of dirt. The child appreciates the tangible world through the intangible imagination, being the sole way we can truly value it. This imagination is so fantastical that the word "childish" was made for it. Yet with this came the notion that imagination was a waste of time. So, I wasted time abundantly, facing the water instead of my bitter sentiments.

A certain walk, however, changed me for the better. I would have kept walking if he hadn't gripped my arm and focused my attention on a winding dirt path made purely by the trodding feet of others. We eased sideways down the earth's façade as loose dirt crumbled with each footstep. The earth transitioned abruptly into broken bricks and rock, eventually blending into the pebbles beneath the water's surface. And then, the shore held its breath. A clearing revealed sand unburdened by tree roots. The noises from the world above met at the threshold of this entrance, sucking the sounds into a vacuum. It relieved our ears, tired from the bustling traffic on the bridge above.

Below, the remains of one tree fell gracefully, clutching onto its stump by a thread. No force, no interference, only the humble submission of the natural fall. A gentle curve developed on the log, becoming the seat we shared. At that point, with the river on either side of you, the world opened wide. The curves of this bend reached out and up, encompassing the layers of the world absolute. The rest blurred behind us into the garrison of trees. The herons flew past with wings stretched wide, revealing blue-hued feathers. A loon dove into the water, resurfacing several yards ahead in seconds. A squirrel flitted among the canopy and bolted along the fallen tree. The branches trembled under its weight and reverberated back to us. Only then was I reminded of the passing of time.

In this alcove of the river, protected by the canopy and the earth as my wall, I rediscover a simplicity I've forgotten. When our backs were to the world, I found myself outside of it. What became my escape from reality transformed into my appreciation for it. This spot along the river that eventually connects to the ocean and the rest of the world—this spot taught me rediscovery. And we rediscovered this spot time after time, witnessing the unencumbered morphosis of the river.

Bill Williams

Chimoio

IAC, Mozambique, 1987.

It's about 10pm and we're just finishing a game of Scrabble. I reassure Mari: "Don't worry if there's a bit of shooting later on—there are occasionally attacks when it's a full moon, but our guys drive them off pretty quickly."

We retire to our rooms in my bungalow, one of twelve houses in the staff accommodation area of the campus.

Half an hour later the sound of bursts of gunfire from the classroom area adjoining the student dormitories wakes me and I notice immediately that our electricity had been cut off. Mari has woken too, and I hasten to assure her that the attackers will quickly be driven off. I avoid mentioning that the fact they managed to cut the electricity wires feeding IAC showed that this time they were unusually well-prepared.

I had been teaching for more than a year as a cooperante (volunteer) at the Instituto Agrário de Chimoio (IAC), an agricultural college in central Mozambique. Mari, a friend and English teacher friend based in the capital Maputo had come to visit, keen to see life in more rural parts of the country.

Apart from Ivanov, an older Bulgarian colleague, I was the only non-Mozambican working at IAC. My Mozambican colleagues and students spoke the local language of whatever part of the country they came from. More than forty distinct languages have been recorded, but we all normally communicated in Portuguese, an inheritance from the former colonial power that the Mozambican government had adopted after independence as the official national language, hoping to avoid dominance by any one ethnic group. All my previous teaching had been in English-speaking countries. So before arriving in Mozambique in 1986 I travelled to Lisbon for a two-month intensive course in Portuguese, just enough to teach chemistry. I was to discover that everyday conversation and badinage between colleagues would take much longer.

Since 1977, a civil war has been waging in Mozambique between RENAMO (backed by Ian Smith before Zimbabwean independence in 1980 and later by the Apartheid government in South Africa) and the FRELIMO government forces.

I had explained to Mari earlier that, although there were regular RENAMO attacks in the area and that the roads were unsafe after nightfall, we at IAC (around 200 students and staff) were protected by a sizeable garrison. Revelling a little in my role as intrepid volunteer teacher working in a war zone, I had told her that I knew of cases where some international workers had been abducted by the RENAMO "bandits" based in Gorongosa, a former National Park some 100 kilometres northeast of our location. I always had sturdy shoes, a tough denim jacket and jeans and a belt with a secret pocket containing a hundred-dollar bill on standby in case things seemed to be going wrong.

The RENAMO forces were reported to be quite well-armed, but they apparently survived with very little in the way of food or even clothes in the bush in Gorongosa, living alongside groups of local people they had kidnapped (the male children often inducted as boy soldiers).

As we watch from a window at the back of the house, I begin to be concerned that the machine-gun fire is continuing longer than usual and is punctuated by what I recognise as mortar rockets and other explosions—probably grenades. Some bullets ricochet off our roof.

We can see what looks like a large bonfire near the dormitories about 500m away. Then, to my relief, things seem to quieten down and we hear a lot of cheering. "Looks like that's all sorted" I reassure Mari.

Then we see what looks like a large crowd moving our way, illuminated by flaming torches held aloft that seem to show a dancing figure in some kind of head-dress in the middle (a curandeiro, or witchdoctor perhaps?). The throng emits an unworldly ululating sound (are there women too?). Stark reality dawns: the attackers have been victorious and are heading towards our quarters.

I hear a rush of footsteps outside and realise that my boss, the Director, and his family, whose bungalow adjoins mine, are making a run for it. But I'm not sure it's safe to run in the dark, especially with a visitor who doesn't know the area. I quickly decide to stay put, knowing the front and back doors are securely locked.

Once the yelling crowd reach the Director's house, we can hear them hammering on the door and then smashing it open and dragging out his belongings—ironically all boxed in crates as he was due to move south next morning. As no lights are working, I tell Mari our best bet is to hide underneath the low-lying double bed in my room. The shouting continues and I realise the yelling mob are now at the back of my house. We hear windows smashing, then some heavy object battering the back door.

Mari seems reasonably calm and, although my knees are trembling, my brain is fully alert. "Right Mari, here we go, under the bed and not a sound." As the smashing continues, we lie on the floor and wiggle under the bed.

There is a sudden burst of gunfire from behind the house and, during what sounds like a fierce exchange of fire, the hammering on the door stops. The firing gradually dies down and, as we strain our ears, we can hear what sounds like the door of the house just behind mine being smashed and a lot more yelling. The sounds then seem to be growing gradually fainter until, finally, silence reigns apart from the habitual night sounds of the crickets.

We crawl out and begin to convince ourselves that it is over and that we appear to have survived unharmed. The only things taken from my house are the curtains from the broken kitchen window—I hear later that they took any material they could find to make clothes back at Gorongosa.

I hadn't smoked a cigarette in ten years. But I light one up from a packet someone had left. It tastes horrible and I hurriedly stub it out again.

After some time, we hear low voices outside and someone whispers cautiously through the door, "Professor Bill?" "*Sim, estou aqui*" (Yes, it's me), I reply and open it to find Jafar, one of our mature students, and another lad with an AK47 automatic rifle on the porch. They are going through all the buildings to check for survivors. The attackers have blown up the school bus and one of the labs with grenades, they tell us. But most of the boys and girls in the dormitories had managed to get out in time.

We learn later that two teenage boy students, a kitchen worker, my colleague Jeremias, an agriculture lecturer from the house behind, and his girlfriend, a student, had all been abducted. There were no deaths or injuries on our side. One of the attackers, a young lad, was wounded in the chest and had been left behind. My chemistry lab had been smashed up and when I go see it the next day, footprints of bare feet are still visible in the white phenol powder that has been spilled onto the floor.

Next day we were all moved to temporary accommodation in Chimoio, the nearest town. IAC was temporarily closed. Mari went to Zimbabwe to fly back to Maputo as the road to the capital was too dangerous to travel.

I realised I needed to think through what my own plans were going to be. My mother, Kal, then in her late sixties, was due to come over from Ireland to visit me at IAC. I didn't want to worry her unduly, but I needed to put off the visit. I queued up at the town post office to make a long-distance call and, over the crackly international line, told her "Things were a bit up and down security-wise" so it was best we postponed the trip for a while. To my relief, she seemed content with that.

A couple of days after the attack, when I was sharing a room in a local boarding school with two Mozambican colleagues from IAC, one of them remarked that there had coincidentally been a TV crew filming a documentary nearby. Hearing of the raid, they had travelled to the college to film the aftermath. When he said it was for Irish TV, I had a horrified vision of my mother settling down in her living room in Cork to watch the evening news and being confronted with graphic footage of the attack and destruction at her eldest son's workplace.

I needed to do something to reassure the mother, so I frantically asked around to find out more about this Irish TV crew. I was told they were still in town, staying in a hotel on the outskirts of Chimoio (the only functioning hotel at that time). I immediately took a taxi there and was relieved to find they were happy to interview me.

My aim was to play down the whole thing and present myself as unscathed and serene about my situation. The one-hour documentary was shown on primetime RTE, the Irish broadcaster, the following week and I had apparently succeeded in my intention as on subsequent long-distance calls Mum seemed to accept the idea that I was fine.

I recently came across the VHS tape that my family recorded from the television at the time. I digitized it and posted it on Youtube. Watching it now, I come across as slightly weird and seem to be speaking with a bit of a Dublin accent—unthinkable for a Cork man, even one who had left Ireland fifteen years previously and had been speaking almost exclusively Portuguese for the previous eighteen months. Could I have been suffering from shock or trauma from the night of the attack?

The video is harrowing in places, accurately depicting the civil war in Mozambique and the destruction caused by RENAMO, which was being sponsored by South Africa's apartheid government.

EPILOGUE

IAC reopened for classes a week later. International Voluntary Service (IVS), the organisation in the UK that sent me to Mozambique, suggested I should pull out, but they eventually accepted my decision to stay on and continue teaching as long as I didn't stay overnight at IAC. I found a flat in Chimoio, IVS sent a sturdy, though rather heavy sit-up-and-beg-style Dutch bicycle and I set out each morning after sun-up at 6:30 to cycle the 12km to IAC, taught my classes and returned each evening before sunset at 6 pm.

Of the abducted people, the two young lads, who were probably more athletic and better fed than their captors, managed to make a dash for freedom the following night as the group trekked through the bush. Eight days later there was another attack on IAC and the kitchen worker they had brought back to guide them also escaped.

When Jeremias was released around a year later during a FRELIMO attack, he returned in a rather traumatized state and spoke of severe shortages of food for everybody in the camp where he was forced to give classes. I never heard anything more of the fate of the girl student.

In the aftermath of the attack I heard it said that, although there was officially a significant garrison of fifty soldiers guarding IAC, at the time there were in fact only twelve to fifteen, and of these most had gone into town for the night.

What probably saved Mari and myself was that, just as they were on the point of smashing their way into my house, the attackers were distracted by the Political Commissar of the garrison (Frelimo followed Soviet military structures, with military ranks being supervised by political ones). The Commissar came round the corner of the house and opened fire with a gun in each hand. The ensuing exchange apparently led to the attackers moving on to the next house and to Jeremias's abduction. The only information I had about our saviour was his rank. I never had an opportunity to meet the man or even find out his name. When I sent a message asking what I could offer him as a reward, word came back that he would like a Bible in Shona (a language spoken in Zimbabwe, but very similar to the local language spoken around Chimoio). These couldn't he bought in Mozambique (no books of any kind were to be found in the province where we were based), but fortuitously I got a lift to Zimbabwe that weekend and managed to bring a copy back and send it to him. When I then tried to set up a meeting to thank him personally, I was told he had been re-stationed to another part of the country.

POSTSCRIPT

It has taken me thirty-three years to decide to write this account of my experience in 1987, although it has remained vivid in my memory ever since. The decision was precipitated by re-watching the RTE documentary. The TV program paints an accurate, and at times disturbing account of the period. I hope here to provide a glimpse of what I learnt of the everyday work and resilience of the students and staff at IAC and other schools who continued to trust and invest in education despite all the chaos and hardship they then faced in this and most other parts of Mozambique.

Barreiro, Portugal, June 2021

Margaret Tseng

Going to the Woods

On a calm winter's day, I went to the woods. I wanted to write, and to live this fraction of my life deliberately.

The freshly fallen snow crunched under my boots as I approached the trail alone, pen and paper in hand. Stopping by the entrance to the woods, I glanced at the posted map, absentmindedly noted the path I would take, and stepped in.

The forest was quiet as I made my way amongst the barren trees. There were no small finches twittering, nor squirrels chattering. Even the usual dog-walkers and hikers were absent. The sounds of human civilization fell away as I moved farther and farther from the buildings at the entrance to the woods. There was only the whoosh of wind in the trees and the soft sound of my footsteps in the crisp, pristine snow.

I had not considered exactly how far to walk before picking a spot to sit and write, and I decided to continue until I found a natural stopping point. So I walked on, passing stout evergreens, imposing but worn-down boulders, and a row of tall shrubs bent above the path like a welcoming canopy for a guest of honor. I crossed the bridge of planks above the mud of the vernal ponds, pausing to contemplate the flat patches of land which were now concealed under snow, but where the water would pool in the spring. All the while, the clouds rushed to their urgent business in the east, prodded by the wind.

I soon arrived at an intersection, which brought to mind a poem that I had studied in ninth grade. "Two roads diverged in a yellow wood, and I . . ." I stopped and chose none of the three paths that lay before me. Instead, I sat down on the log at the base of the signpost and unfolded my paper.

I clicked my pen and stared into the brown mass of tree trunks. Their bare forms pointed, like admiring fingers, to the sky. Looking up, I saw the clouds gliding past and watched their shadows rippling on the ground. Somehow, I had never noticed this effect before, and I marveled at how the shadows seemed to traverse the gently sloping hills of the land at varying speeds. I made a note on my paper.

My thoughts turned to my sensory perceptions, and I scribbled down a brief summary. The woods enveloped me in a brown-blue-white landscape, and the air was fresh and sweet. An insistent insect buzzed in my ears before giving up. Although I hadn't perceived any animals earlier, I could now hear the distant calls of blue jays and starlings. Without the distraction of my phone or other people, I was finding the woods to be an experience in itself.

I remembered my impetus to go to the woods alone. As part of our studies on Transcendentalism, my class had been tasked with visiting the woods and writing a journal entry there, staying for an hour without interacting with other people. We read the works of Emerson and Thoreau beforehand and identified quotes that represented the key ideas of the writings. The curious sentences and turns of phrase passed through my mind as I sat in the woods.

I recalled Emerson's metaphor of the "transparent eyeball" from his essay "Nature." Like the eyeball, I sought to see the world around me without being a disturbance. On this visit to the woods, I felt I was seeing Nature for the first time. As I observed the natural scene, I felt the separation between myself and the natural world weaken. The quiet serenity of the forest filled my mind.

Emerson and Thoreau also wrote extensively about the influence of society on the individual. In his essay "Self-Reliance," Emerson extolled the virtues of originality over conformity and lamented the loss of individuality in people who only followed societal norms. I contemplated how much of my own personality had been shaped by those around me and wondered how much of it was a good thing.

The Transcendentalist explanations of the constant self-repression caused by societal judgment had resonated with me in the classroom. But here in the woods, alone with my own thoughts and my pen, I felt free. I began writing again in earnest, jotting down every thought, sketching every picture that I wanted to express. There was no one to stop me from being my own self.

Roísín Leggett Bohan

Everything Possible Happens Somewhere

The rain fell like liquid mirrors dipped in neon. The wipers not taking a breath. I dropped him off at the bus stop on the Grand Parade. An abandoned umbrella lay in half-mast on the ground. I hardly knew the man—and didn't know yet how he would shape my future. His name was Alan Egan.

It all started with a forgotten cap. I found it lying on the car floor amongst the dog hair tumbleweed. It was faded, damp, and denim. I had joined the writers group the previous month. Alan was one of the esteemed organisers. I was beside myself with trepidation the first time I turned up. I had read that one of their members had won a short story award. These were published authors and I was an imposter. But somewhere hanging in the ether, courage was floating free of charge—so I plucked it and said to myself, I'll give one meeting a go. The fact that I had made it to the shortlist of a short story competition a year before, (the first one I had ever entered) fostered my daring.

I think of the myriad of eventualities that make the pattern of life. What if I hadn't written that short story? Hadn't been shortlisted? Hadn't turned up at the writers group? What if it hadn't been raining. What if I hadn't offered Alan a lift? What if he had said "No, you're grand, I'll walk instead." Then I wouldn't have heard him say, "Your writing is worth something," and I wouldn't have felt like there was a moth flapping its powder-wings in my stomach and I wouldn't have started to believe in my work and more importantly, I wouldn't be where I am now.

> 05-10-18
> Hi Róisín, and please forgive me for writing
> from my personal email address.
> Three things.

#1 Many thanks again for the lift.
#2 The Bridport Prize is the name that I couldn't recall—it came to me while on the bus. As I said, you have a talent, a gift. Your writing grabs the reader—powerful, stark, emotive and real, while also being multi-layered and packed with imagery. Submit. Aim high.
#3. It is vaguely possible that I left a battered old denim cap in your car. Sentimental value only (it comes from a previous generation). If you do happen to find it, maybe hang on to it for me?
Thanks again,
Alan
P.S. Should have accepted your extended lift offer. The bus was mad late, but at least I remembered Bridport.

06-10-18
Hi Alan,
Good to hear from you.
#1 You are more than welcome.
#2 I remember seeing the Bridport prize pop up on my searches from time to time, it is rather prestigious. I really value your words of encouragement and I will endeavour to limber up for some serious high aims.
#3 Old denim battered cap intact and awaiting your noble *ceann*. I cannot lie, there were tears, your cap wasn't the same when you left it on the dog haired floor of my car. Acute separation anxiety. I gave it a good pep talk though and a cup of hot chocolate (with marshmallows). You'll be glad to hear it is doing fine this morning and is settling in to its new although temporary abode.

Best,
Róisín
P. S. Mad late buses should not be allowed,
bring back the tram!

And so, the cap was returned to its owner and with-it a friendship was founded. Long walks through the city of Cork ensued accompanied by animated conversations. We talked of philosophy, writing, and the love and loss of dogs. I often found myself bent over in laughter at his witty observations of life. We continued to critique our work when the writer's group folded and through him, I became to realize that my writing was valuable. He is for me the character in Bryan McMahon's short story "The Windows of Wonder"—the man unfolding his cupped hands to reveal two butterflies, the butterflies are still for a moment, dazed by sunlight, and then, as if brushed with life, they beat their velvet wings and take flight, creating a pattern all their own.

When you are hypersensitive, you live with the constant murmuration of the inner critic—I held an inherited belief that I wasn't worthy, not even walking through University College Cork campus to take a shortcut. I had always thought that people who attended university were made of much better stuff than me. My father owned a grocery shop in Cork's suburbs. From an early age I worked in that shop. On my lunch breaks in primary school, I would sprint down the laurel hedged road, stand at the counter in my uniform and wrap a Cuthbert's sliced pan, a bag of ten cola bottles, or serve twenty Rothmans depending on the customer. I was the second last child of seven and the idea of attending college was never entertained. To obtain a job, to be able to support oneself, that was the expectation. Not that my father and mother weren't educated. My father had a great love of reading and was a talented storyteller. My mother was artistic and could have become a great writer if she had believed in herself. Although I did attend Homerton College in Cambridge to attain a degree in health studies, it was for pure practical reasons and led to a career in nursing—it did not feed my soul.

My lack of self-belief clung to me like a sticky back from my days in secondary school. There was one incident that framed my self-doubt. My English teacher was short, stern, and dramatic. I liked her. On one occasion she was handing back our homework and said she was disappointed by the short stories. Then she raised her small hand, that barely peaked through the arms of her purple shawl and said, "The only person that will get into the honours class is Róisín Leggett." She planted my copy onto to the desk in front of me. "Very well done Róisín, unique style, great pacing, wonderful dialogue." I was stunned, my cheeks began to burn. I felt validated, elated. A month later my English teacher went on sick-leave and didn't return for the remainder of the year. She was replaced by a substitute who was apathetic, pale, and monotone. I didn't like her. She called out from a list, the names of pupils she had selected for the honours class. I was not on the list, and I didn't say a thing. I was devastated but told no one.

Living with hypersensitivity is like carrying an invisible weight—no one can see it. You hear, see, smell and touch in a heightened way—as if everything around you seeps into your core. When you walk into a room you hear everything at once—the low hum of a radiator, a fluorescent light that blinks on and off. You hear the clang of a spoon drop to the floor from twelve feet away. You are too sensitive. This was the constant refrain when I was growing up and so I began to view sensitivity as a negative trait. I absorbed everything, every word that was said, every facial expression, every full-throated laugh, and every unsaid loss. But by writing I began to assimilate these emotions through my characters' voices—and now, I see its purpose in every freckle that ignites my skin and in every sentence that I craft.

Alan knew of my longing to pursue the MA in Creative Writing and so he began the process of desensitization. He portioned out our meetings with walks through the UCC campus, lunch in the main student canteen and coffee in the café where the tutors frequented. I was becoming acclimatized to the environment. It was frightening and thrilling all at the same time.

Alan became a tutor in UCC for some time after obtaining

his primary and master's degree there. His passion for education and Cork's history makes perfect sense considering his lineage. I remember meeting him on the Alumni bridge where the willow dips its leaves in River Lee. He pointed to the main gates of the college with his umbrella. "You see those gates, my grandfather believed that every person, regardless of their background, had a right to walk through those gates and be entitled to a university education." Alan's grandfather, Michael Egan, became involved in the trade union movement in the early 1900s and worked tirelessly to improve the employment conditions and education of Cork's inhabitants. He organised a series of free lectures for the working people of Cork, with his friend Alfred O'Rahilly, (later to be President of UCC). In 1916 he featured at a conference in UCC, in which he spoke of his heartfelt wish—that the workers of Cork would lose their terror of the university, and that it would no longer be seen as place where only "the privileged" could attend. Although Alan has no memory of his grandfather, (he died when Alan was an infant) I believe that his message has been sieved down through the portals of time to his grandson. The present has inherited the past and now I walk through the gates of UCC with a knapsack on my back and a story on my mind.

And so, it is has been almost three years since that wet and windy evening when I found a weathered denim cap on the floor of my car. And, at the time of writing this I am in middle of writing my thesis for my MA in Creative Writing in UCC. I was recently notified that a poem of mine will be featured in the Cork's Poetry in the Park series. And this is how Alan replied:

> -Yo there Róisín the writer . . .
> Yes, brilliant news about your poetry in the park.
> Tell me this . . .
> How do the wise and the aged ones get to see/
> hear/feel your words?
> Do bells ring out, do trees speak, do town criers
> shout oyez, oyez as they wander the confines,
> unfurling manuscripts as crowds gather, does

> perchance an aeroplane fly overhead on the
> hour, writing a multi-coloured vapour stanza
> in the sky?

I am indebted to Alan Egan for his belief in my ability. His phrase, which he reminds me of over and over—"Everything possible happens somewhere," has threaded its way into my mind like a tapestry. He still whoops and cheers when he hears I received a first-class honour on an assignment. Do I still feel like an imposter? Yes. But now, when I do, I just settle down to write and the scythe in my mind divides the chasms of insecurity so I can let the doubt go. And where there is a letting-go there is always something to say.

Tadhg Carey

Standing in the Dome of Hades

On the crest of the hill, the world whispers in full voice; every breath, every tempestuous moment, every renting cry! It's five a.m., and my insomnia visits me with a call from Hades. I am impotent, standing in the open mouth of the window, as he rises and bays wildly at the hill, reveling in this temporary release and howling with all his might; as if in fretful knowledge that soon daylight will return, and all his blackness, all his seething beauty, will once again be banished to the depths below.

Not strong enough on this night to illuminate the large expanse of sea hemmed in by this great harbour off to the south, still some of the lights on the small island, across the short channel below, reach out in a flickering protest at this growing onslaught. Now, where we stand, Hades fury has ascended. It has risen to its farthest reaches, but the world above will allow him rise no higher than the confines of this grey dome in which we are now entrapped. It has closed in about us, containing everything. Within it, all his anger whips past my window, punishing the harried streaks of rain that are now cast as grey sheets against the backdrop of the all but occluded lights reaching out to me through the angry night. Stretched to their limits, these sheets race as an infinity of endless threads, squeezed into ever accelerating circles; fretful, frantically seeking to escape the anger that drives them, and desperate to breach the confines of this angry dome that has ascended in the night.

Here, high up on the hill, my tall and slender beauty holds fast before me. Silhouetted now in this deathly darkness, the sequins of her gown are all but torn from their threads, glistening randomly as they catch occasional sparks; the flickering reflections of the smothered light reaching up from the island below. She is deluged and harried endlessly, but she fights furiously. It is a struggle to prevail, all her elegance and poise stripped bare. He is relentless and any struggle to maintain her pristine lines, to stand with dignity, is utterly fruitless. His raging gale stretches ever higher, until now he is a storm, and so he rips through her clusters of leaves, bending her slim figure ever further; wrenching and tearing at her in the hope that she will relent, that finally she can take no more. Then, in defiance, she springs back once again. This frantic dance before me is no choreographed and gracefully tragic pas-de-deux. This is real! It is become a street fight. Hades, now furiously whipping sheets of water across her flanks, is determined to have his way, to rip her from the ground. If Hades cannot rise up and escape this seething domed-world, then he will take a prize. He will drag this beauty by the hair and tear her from her roots and down into his depths below. But no! She is young and slim and strong; and she fights, and this furious brute will not have his way. As a lithe and flexible mast, she bends and sways, and defiantly shrugs off the best that Hades brings. He will not take her! But he will take something. Hades always takes something! Suddenly, as she snaps back once again, a young branch is ripped from her and vanishes with him into his darkness. My heart freezes, and in this moment something in me also dies.

But when it is over, I know that she will still stand tall and elegant in the morning light; and I will find her once again swaying sensuously, clad in her elegant green sequined gown. This past night's anguish reaches into both our souls, and I know that there is nothing to do but stand within its cold embrace, until night passes slowly into light. And when it comes, I will again feel the sunlight warm upon my face; and I too will sway with her, gently in the breeze.

Sonja Murphy

Jumping Back in Time

In my earliest memory, I am learning something. I am with my parents in my neighbour's boat—which is a rowboat in my mind, even though it was a speedboat in reality—and we are rowing. We arrive at the base of a cliff. At the top, there is a crowd of people, all dressed in costumes. They each take turns jumping into the water. In other boats, people laugh and take pictures. The sun is on my face, it is summer in Sweden, and I am three. The next diver comes forward. He is a big yellow bird, and when he jumps, the sunlight catches on all of his feathers, he flaps his arms, and it looks like he really is flying. For a moment. He crashes into the water. He surfaces with his feathers all soaked and he swims to shore. Already, even seconds after it happened, I am wanting to see it again. I am about to learn that it is impossible to make time bend back over itself.

This memory changes whenever I revisit it, which is often. Sometimes the divers stand on the top of a cliff, and other times at the end of a pier. Sometimes there are dozens of other boats watching them, sometimes it is only us. If you were to give me back those five seconds, if I was to see it for a second time, I would remember every detail. Or so I tell myself.

Back then, all I wanted was to see the yellow bird diving again. But we were getting further from the cliffs, we were sailing home, and I'd only seen it happen once. I asked to go back to the divers. My neighbour said that it was over now. The divers were gone. I told her to bring them back, and she said that was impossible. Until that moment, I must have assumed that turning back time was within the seemingly infinite power of adults. But apparently it wasn't. Time now revealed itself to be a straight line, and each moment seemed incredibly fragile, incredibly dangerous, since they can never be redone. Fueled by a kind of senseless rage accessible only to toddlers, I picked up a plastic bottle and threw it at her. I missed, and it landed in the water. It might still be there today. Even though I lived it, what I felt in that moment is as inaccessible to me now as what the Alexandrians might've felt when they watched their library burn. Either way, I hope I was ashamed. It was an awkward journey home. I sat, watching the water curl around the boat, with my new revelation. The past cannot be relived.

Sometimes, the memory seemed too perfect to be real. When I ask my parents about that day, they can only remember the horror they felt when I threw the bottle at our neighbour. Doubting my own past, I tried, for hours, to find something about this cliff diving online. With the help of Google translate, I found an archive of a local newspaper. There was an article, from 2003, about the dives. Several blurry pictures were attached. Four divers, with their arms around each other, and the bird was in the middle, feathers soaking wet. His mask was off and he was smiling. Their names were written below. I searched for him on Facebook, filled with nonsense notions of messaging him to tell him about the role that he accidentally played in my earliest and most important memory, and I found his account. He hadn't posted in years, but his friends had been leaving comments on his page regularly. I translated them from Swedish. He'd since died. So it goes. In that moment, I felt that I hadn't changed at all from when I wanted to rewind time to watch the yellow bird jump again. Because what had I hoped to gain from any of this, if not some form of time travel?

Whenever I finish reading a book, I expect to eventually re-read it. The thought of only experiencing something once and then never again is painful to me. If I were to actually do this, if I were to never read a book just once, what kind of a future would I have? In my old age, would I be stuck circling around my books, pulling out ones with yellowed pages, reading them all again, sacrificing new experiences in a failed attempt to replicate the past?

Sometimes I feel the same way about everything, and I wonder when my first life lesson will start to sink in.

The past cannot be relived. We take for granted how hard that is to learn. I've watched others come to this realisation. As children, my friends and I once chased a fox and her cubs through a field. The foxes got back into their den, but one of my friends, unable to let go of the moment, reached in and grabbed the fox's tail. She got bitten. And a decade later, as secondary school came to an end, my friends and I sat on the wall behind the school, each of us silently realising that we'd never do it again. But a few days later, during our final exams, I saw one of my friends sitting on the wall by herself, and then she got off, dejected, probably realising that it would never be the same.

The past cannot be relived. I can't think of any lesson more worth learning. At first, it may seem painful, but the pain is nothing compared to what comes before it: the euphoric joy of never wanting this moment to pass. It's a lesson that has to be learned again and again, but I'm grateful that my education in transience began so early. Because of this, the few days of Summer seem brighter, late-night conversations are more keenly felt, and when I laugh, I stretch out the sound. Almost everything I have now is temporary. There is joy in every moment, and it is made stronger by knowing that it won't last. When I walk my dog, I feel every one of her fourteen years. At some point in the future, these daily walks will be as blurry and indistinct as my first memory, as surreal as watching a man dressed as a bird diving off a cliff. I love them all the more for that.

Phil Terrana

Never Mess With a Nun Named Leo

Life has a tendency to turn on a dime. At the end of seventh grade, my first year at St. Francis Xavier, I received the Daughters of the American Revolution Good Citizens award. Sometimes being the new kid on the block, the unknown, has its advantages.

By the next year, that award was old news.

It began as a casual observation, thrown out in haste, and obviously, with little or no thought given to the consequences. After spending most of the afternoon standing in the back of the room as punishment, my three classmates and I had been called to our teacher's desk to explain our continued misbehavior. Had we shown a sufficient degree of remorse, apologized, and promised it wouldn't happen again, we could have been on our way, but instead we chose to dig that hole that our parents had always warned us about.

The question was a very simple one.

"What do you boys think you're doing?"

Schoolboys have been asked this question for ages, and the correct response has always been the same. Look down at your feet, shuffle them around a little, shrug your shoulders, shake your head from side to side and then say, "I dunno."

That is the only acceptable answer. No one really expects you to incriminate yourself. "What do you boys think you're doing?" has never been a question in search of an answer, but rather a rhetorical assertion that whatever you were doing—and no one really needs an explanation—but whatever it was, was the wrong thing to be doing.

Our teacher was only interested in getting that question out of the way in order to move on to the punishment phase. The request was a formality, an icebreaker as if school were a social event, and breaking the rules of a party game to be treated as such. Smart kids know this. Of course, smart kids don't get in trouble.

I accept much of the blame for what happened next because I was the one who responded to her inquiry. My foolish comeback didn't even answer the question she had posed, but reluctantly, students don't get do-overs in the classroom the way they do on the playground.

"The other eighth grade is better than ours," I said, in response to the question, "What do you boys think you're doing?"

That was our answer as if to imply that whatever it was that we boys were doing, we were doing because we were in the wrong eighth grade, and if we were in the right eighth grade, we wouldn't be doing it. The truth is, we were very happy in her eighth grade and got along well with our classmates. We were simply looking for someone else to blame for our bad behavior.

"What do you mean?" our teacher asked, appearing honestly confused, but actually just handing us a bigger shovel to dig an even bigger hole.

The four of us, taking turns and answering in bits and pieces, and starts and stumbles, were able to convey the vague suggestion that the other eighth-grade teacher was fairer, more fun, more understanding, and that the other eighth grade got along better with their teacher, learned more, and enjoyed themselves more.

Now would be a good time to make clear that we were not just talking to an eighth-grade teacher, but rather to the eighth-grade teacher who also happened to be the principal. Equally important, we were students in Saint Francis Xavier Elementary School, and the teacher/principal happened to also be a nun named Sister Leo Marie.

I don't think enough consideration is given to the thought process that a nun goes through in choosing a name. Our birth names are given to us and we learn to live with them. I like to think we all eventually grow into our names by making whatever adjustments are needed to make the names work. However, when a person is given the opportunity to choose their own name—well, I think the name they choose says something about them.

St. Leo, a theological scholar and the first Pope to be called

"The Great," had been pope for twenty-one years when he died at the age of sixty-one, which in the fifth century was a lifetime and then some. These are great—no pun intended—accomplishments, but Pope Leo is best remembered for meeting Attila the Hun at the gates of Rome in 452 and persuading him to turn back from his invasion of Italy at a time when the Vandals were conquering the entire civilized world and the Roman Empire was in rapid decline.

So there you have it. Our teacher chose the name Leo, after St. Leo, the only man in history to have ever gotten the upper hand on Attila the Hun. I didn't know these facts at the time, didn't realize the significance of her name choice. I just thought Leo was a weird name for a girl.

Nevertheless, when she could have chosen any name in the book, she chose the name of one of history's great leaders, and I chose to tell her that the other eighth-grade teacher was better than her.

For a moment, she didn't say anything and neither did we. For all our missteps, finally, we knew enough to shut up.

We waited, and waited, and waited.

Finally, she spoke.

"Well," she said, "it seems to me that if the other eighth grade is better, the other eighth-grade teacher is better, and you can learn more in the other eighth grade, then by all means you should go to the other eighth grade.

"I want you boys to bring all your books and papers home, and when you return on Monday, go over to the other eighth grade and ask if she'd be willing to let you join her class."

Wow! We looked at each other in disbelief. That was definitely better than we had expected.

Her plan sounded reasonable enough, although we should have been suspicious. Sister Leo Marie was the principal and certainly didn't need the other teacher's approval. Everyone, including the other nuns, did what Sister Leo Marie told them to do—except for the four of us, of course.

Likewise, if she was sending us over there, why did we even have to ask if it was okay? These were both good questions, but we were too busy savoring our victory to ask them.

We packed our books and left the room. Outside, we convinced each other that we had done the right thing. We really did think that the other eighth grade was better. Not only that, but when word got out that we had actually stood up to Sister Leo Marie—not just stood up to her, but actually gotten the better of her, well we would be heroes of sorts.

I lived in a different parish from the other three boys, so while each of them had short five- or ten-minute walks, I was looking at about an eight-block walk to catch a city bus, and then another three- or four-block walk before I'd be home. I said goodbye to my buddies and began my trek home, using the whole twenty-minute bus ride home to figure out a way to sneak my stuff into the house without my parents knowing, and make sure it stayed hidden all weekend.

We had a lot of books in those days, and I'd never once brought this many books home in the middle of the school year. In addition to the books, I had notebooks, binders, pencils, rulers, and loose papers stashed in my shirt and pockets, as backpacks were very much non-existent in 1960. We still carried everything on our hips or bundled in our arms. My supposed victory over Sister Leo Marie seemed to literally have come with a lot of unforeseen baggage.

If I was successful in sneaking my books into the house, I'd have the whole weekend to devise a plan for getting them out of the house on Monday.

In spite of the difficulties, I actually thought I'd succeeded with my ruse when I put the last book under the bed. Unfortunately, I didn't suspect then what I know now. You can't sneak anything past your parents. If you think you have, it is only because they are letting you think that. In this particular case, my mother chose not to let it ride, and I had to come clean with the whole story—a story, not the story.

I explained how some new kids had come to our class and it wasn't until they were already in the room that the teacher discovered we didn't have enough seats. Rather than make the new kids, who had already moved once, move a second time, the teacher asked for volunteers to go to the other eighth grade and a couple of us said we didn't mind. Since it was late in the day, we just decided to bring everything home for the weekend and start fresh on Monday. It seemed like the right thing to do, I added—still digging.

"What did you do to get in trouble?" My mother asked.

Sometimes, when you're a kid, it's a waste of time to even try to come up with a good lie because no one seems to appreciate the effort.

So, I told her the truth—what I had said to Sister Leo Marie and what Sister Leo Marie had said to us—and she took it surprisingly well.

Seemed all the adults were taking remarkably well, what I was throwing out, but those were trusting times. We hadn't yet become a society that questioned everyone's motives or were suspicious of everyone's actions. I was probably just a tad guilty myself of accepting everyone else's acceptance. I should have been asking myself a few questions.

"Well, we'll see what happens," was all Mom said.

The good news about having been discovered so quickly the previous Friday was that I didn't have to worry about sneaking everything out on Monday. My mother helped me gather my books and was encouraging as she said goodbye. I supposed she could have driven me to school rather than have me take the bus, but this was, after all, still my mess. The good news was that it would soon be over.

The four of us met in front of our new eighth grade, which happened to be in a different building, atop a flight of stairs. We were excited about meeting our new classmates and our new teacher, who had undoubtedly been made aware of all the praise we had showered upon her. At the sound of the bell, the class marched in and took their seats. When they were all in the room, our new teacher saw us out of the corner of her eye as she was about to close the door, paused and slowly approached us.

"Can I help you boys?"

"Sister Leo Marie sent us over to ask if we could be in your class," we all mumbled, saying no more than what we thought we had to say.

"Visit for just the day?" she asked, sounding very confused.

"No, Sister. Every day. We want to transfer to your eighth grade."

Sister Anonymous—I don't even remember her name, which is strange considering just a few days earlier I had claimed she was the best teacher, but she looked at us as she would an Avon Lady turning up at the convent door to sell cosmetics.

"I see," she said, which was a little less than we were expecting.

Again, just as it had been with Sister Leo Marie, we knew we had said enough and hers would be the next words spoken. We just didn't know when they would come.

Nuns had a wonderful way of making you wait—not just wait, but also squirm and sweat while waiting. We never knew what they would do or say because nuns weren't from our world, and so, whatever they did do or say always caught us off guard.

I never really understood nuns. I'm not sure if our parents or even the priests did. I'm not sure the nuns understood each other. They were obviously very, very good women, dedicated women who had only our best interest at heart. But they could seem very vindictive at times, almost relishing the fear they instilled in vulnerable children, and they could really hurt you with those paddles, razor-sharp rulers, and God knows what else they had hidden under those habits—habits, what kind of a name is that for a dress?

At times, they could be very silly and fun-loving. I knew a nun who once got slightly inebriated, in our own house for God's sake, but for the most part nuns were uncommonly serious. They were capable of staring us down from the other end of the pew in a way that'd send chills up and down our spines and convince us that our life on earth was nothing more than a rest stop on the road to eternal damnation. In a world where everyone and everything has its place, nuns were sort of out there in no man's land.

Fully aware of what we were up against, we waited in silence, and continued to wait until finally, she spoke.

"I'm going to have to think it over, boys. Why don't you sit down out here on the steps, and as soon as I've made a decision, I'll let you know."

Maybe we had sprung this on her rather suddenly, but the whole matter didn't seem that complicated to us—certainly not so complicated that it would take her three days to arrive at her decision, but that turned out to be the case.

Three days that we had to sit on those steps, three days that I had to carry my books home on the bus and return with the next day, three days that I had to invent newer and bigger lies to tell my mother. Even the bus driver and other passengers were beginning to wonder what was going on.

For three days, we sat outside what we had hoped would be our new classroom, only to have to explain what we didn't understand ourselves to everyone that walked by—including Monsignor on several occasions. Worst of all, we couldn't figure out what this nun had against us. After all, we had chosen her because she was the best teacher and her eighth grade the better one. Our anger and frustration with her was building.

She wasn't playing fair. Students from both eighth grade classes were joking us, and she didn't seem to care. By the third day, we were mad as hell at her and at each other. I was even mad at the bus driver for the cynical look he gave me every day I took my seat on his bus. We decided we wouldn't want to be in her eighth grade if it were the last eighth grade on earth, which it practically was. Then, just as Sister Leo Marie's class was starting to look better, a miracle happened, maybe not a miracle, but something that caught us completely off guard.

"Okay, boys," she said on the morning of the fourth day, "I think it would be all right for you to join our class. Please come in and find some seats."

Four days. Jesus only needed three days to rise from the dead, but we needed four days just to switch classrooms. Even the Baltimore Catechism couldn't explain that one, and it always had an answer for everything.

The four of us looked at each other, speechless. Just when we were ready to go back even though we doubted we could, we suddenly learned we'd been accepted where we'd finally decided we no longer wanted to be.

Those diabolical nuns were sticking it to us as sure as Lucifer would one day be poking us with his pitchfork in the depths of Hell—if the nuns had anything to say about it. Around this time, it dawned on us that these nuns lived in the same house together, ate their meals sitting around the same table, and had probably been planning their whole strategy while we were sitting on the steps for three days. Maybe diabolical was too good a word.

Inside her class, we discovered we were the heroes that we had expected to be almost a week earlier—sort of. Actually, we were more like novelty items, which was still satisfying for four eighth-grade refugees that no one seemed to want.

There were two cute twins in my new class. I think one of them kind of liked me because she was giving me the eye, which in my unique situation was like two girls giving me the eye, since I didn't have a clue how to tell them apart. Had I been in their class from day one, this might not have been a problem, but by this stage, all kinds of "what ifs" and "if only" were floating through my head.

For the first few days, things couldn't have been better, but the initial excitement over our arrival in their class quickly subsided, and it wasn't long before we became less a novelty and more of a joke.

We discovered that just because two classes teach the same material and finish at the same point in June, didn't mean they are necessarily at the same point on any given day in any given week during the school year. Furthermore, we had just spent the better part of a week sitting on the steps not being taught anything, so we were a little bit out of sync, out of touch, and soon to discover out of luck.

More and more, Sister Heartless chose us—even when our hands weren't raised, to answer questions we didn't know the answers to.

More and more, we were sent to the blackboard to solve math

problems we didn't understand.

More and more, our new classmates were snickering behind our backs, and more and more, we began regretting the situation we'd created.

The twin had even stopped giving me the eye, which since I still didn't know one from the other was like being dumped twice.

Doing the right thing is something thirteen-year-olds generally shy away from, but after a week of making fools of ourselves, we had no choice.

The four of us got together after class one day and headed over to Sister Leo Marie's classroom. We'd been upfront and honest, with her a few weeks ago—to a fault and to our detriment, and we now hoped that a sort of bond born out of mutual respect would lead her to reconsider her punishment—and make no mistake, we now knew we were being punished by a master.

Who were we kidding? Mutual respect had nothing to do with it. We were begging for our old desks back and that was all there was to it.

"Sister," we said, meekly and respectfully like the little choirboys that we were not, "if it would be all right with you, we think we'd like to come back to your class."

"What's wrong?"

"It's just not working out. We were wrong. We made a mistake."

This is where Sister Leo Marie really surprised us. We were ready for another long waiting period, fully expecting now to sit outside her room—our ex-room, for a week, or however long it took. We had taken all our books with us in anticipation of having to bring them home again. We were even prepared for expulsion since there were only two eighth grades and we had pretty much declared we didn't like either one.

"I suppose if you want your old seats back, we can do that. Is that what you want?"

Boy did we! We were back with our old classmates the very next day—novelties again, but now in a nice way.

We realized we'd made a terrible mistake, but she never mentioned the incident. We didn't talk about it either. A decade later, at the Military Entrance Processing Station in Buffalo, I ran into one of my partners in crime, and even then, neither of us spoke about the week Sister Leo Marie taught us a lesson we'd never forget.

She had barely spoken a word during the incident, and nothing afterwards, but had clearly demonstrated who was boss, and who the best teacher was.

We also learned an important history lesson. We learned how Attila the Hun must have felt when he came up against the other Leo.

Rehan Ali

Those Who Knocked on Room 39

Big black gates. They were the first thing I saw coming out of the arch of Chapel St. Right opposite me. Following in the footsteps of my mother and my two older siblings, I didn't realise that behind those gates would exist my home. The prison within which my childhood remains. I buried it there before I left.

It's an odd system. Right in the middle of an old, traditional Irish town. Almost out of nowhere emerges an ecosystem of diversity, of colour. A world of its own. A Direct Provision centre. It is where refugees, asylum seekers, and immigrants gather and lay down their troubles in the pleasure of each other's company. Perhaps the only pleasure that exists behind those gates. It is where they will wait for a decision to be made. A decision about their fate. One that may decide whether they live or not.

Bridgewater House. That was the name given to this centre. Sitting in the middle of Carrick-on-Suir, a small town caught in the path of the River Suir. Ironically, Bridgwater house was previously Saint Joseph's Convent of Mercy. Mercy? It's unfortunate how funny I find that.

The gates were tall. Keeping people out. Keeping people in. My mother had travelled all the way from Pakistan to a country that she didn't even know existed only a few months earlier all to grant her children the further she believed we deserved. Safety, education, opportunity, respect. Now at the foot of the gates, our journey to obtain such a life was only just beginning.

Creaking. The automation of the doors opened up a new world. Slowly walking in, hiding behind the shadow of my mother, I clutched onto my backpack. Altogether we probably had 5 bags containing the only remnants of our past. One for each year of my life. We walked down the sloping driveway towards the main door of the Direct Provision hostel, which was inside a protruding conservatory. The hostel was large, a pale orange brick building. It even looked sickly. When we finally entered the building itself, my mother let out a sigh as she put down our luggage and approached the glass window of the reception.

That's when I saw him. A boy. From China. He was standing at the bottom of a flight of stairs. I got my first lesson there and then. When our eyes met, they stayed there. And then, he ran. Right up the stairs. Inexplicably, I ran too. I was shy. I was confused. I was scared. But I ran too.

I followed him deep into the hostel. Zoomed up many stairs. Dashed through the maze-like hallways and corridors. I remember running that day as if I was in a dream-like state. Catching quick glimpses of my surroundings. Even at that age, I was struck by the uniqueness of this place. I knew it was special. Each floor opened up a new continent. Moving from one hallway to the next felt like moving countries. Each one unique with a certain type of music pouring out of the doors. I knew this music wasn't mine. But I took it. Each corridor emanating the smell of food cooking. Food I had never had before. But I knew now I would. Each room bursting with a conversation in a tongue I could not understand. But I wish I could.

Was this magic? Was the boy that I was chasing teleporting me to different realms of some fantasy land? It sounds childish. But that's what I was after all. Every now and again he would turn back to look at me. As if to check whether I was still there. Was he trying to show me the landscape of my new home? Well, what an introduction. To this day I still wonder if he was truly giving me my first tour? A job I myself would carry out for the next ten years.

During my impromptu orientation, I remember zooming past many numbers. 8, 17, 24, 31, and then 39. Room 39 on the top floor. Hidden in the side of a particularly dark corridor. A fluorescent bulb would erratically flash to light up the reflective digits. Little did I know then that 39 would symbolize my childhood. The golden numbers nailed on the door behind which I would go on to live out my life.

When we had first arrived, the manager had informed my

mother that dinner service had just ended. But there were still some chips left. So, when I rejoined my family, we sat down at a table in the cafeteria and had our meal. As I reached for some ketchup the same boy simply looked at me and shook his head disapprovingly. He was giving me a warning. But I loved ketchup, so I paid no heed to his message of caution. But it wasn't long before I was wishing I did. Sour and bitter. Not like any ketchup I had tasted before. Another lesson I learned quickly. My first day was proving to be quite educational. It was long before I ever had ketchup again.

After trying to eat we were shown to our room. Room 39. A small room with a small window. Was the window out of grace? Or was it to salt our wounds? Showing us what freedom looks like, behind the thin, cracked pane of glass. Well, this is where I'll grow up. Of course, I didn't know that at the time.

I spent so many of my early days with that boy. All of them in fact. His name? I couldn't say. One day I woke up and he was gone. Where did he go? God knows. That was the first time that a friend had been ripped away from me. Unfortunately, it was far from the last. But thank you. For giving me my very first lesson. And for being my very first best friend.

Slowly the days went by. My mother didn't know how long we'd be here, but she had hope. "Not long," she'd say. "We'll be allowed to live in this country and then we can finally be free." The days went by. I don't completely remember those early days embedded into early 2005. I can only recall that year through some key moments. Moving to a new country. Moving to a hostel. And my first day of school in Ireland.

It was at school that I met him. Ose. He lived where I did. We shared the same building. The same "home." But I met him for the first time at school. He was in my class. In senior infants. It didn't take long for us to become friends.

He was from Nigeria. He lived with his mom and a younger brother. A floor under where I was. Every morning he'd knock on our door, door number 39. We'd walk to school together. He was always ready before me. I always looked forward to hearing that knock. We'd travel together. Sit next to each other. Have lunch together. Walk home together. Do our homework together. And then we'd play together. That was life. We only had each other but it was sufficient. In a crowd of children at school, he was the only one that I felt like I could truly be myself around. It's the connection that can only exist between two people who know what life under Direct Provision is like. Even early on, I knew where I lived made me different. It made him different too. We could be different together.

Naruto. He loved Naruto. I liked Beyblade. So, we would take turns controlling the tv room. When and if it was free of course. There was only one after all for all the residents. During one Saturday free from school and the work that accompanied it we were lucky to get the TV room all to ourselves. We watched *The Adventures of Sharkboy and Lavagirl*. That movie will always remind me of him.

Ose was the eldest in his family. He took great care of his younger brother. Always watched out for him. I was the youngest in my family, so I never really had someone to care for. But by watching him he taught me what it meant to care for others. It was a good thing he knew how since his mother was pregnant. She was a kind, gentle woman. I would sometimes go to his room and we'd play his video games. They were all pretty old, like a knock-off Sega Genesis with the games built-in. But it was still a treat. She would pop in with some sandwiches now and again. Pretty simple really. Strawberry jam and butter. They tasted far better than the food in the cafeteria.

I had never really met a pregnant woman before. I know that sounds odd but at my age, it was simply true. It took a while to wrap my mind around the whole concept. A child growing inside of someone. It seemed more like magic than a simple fact of life. A kind of frightening magic if I am to be honest. In fact, for quite a while I was certain that I was being made a fool of. But his mother sure was getting bigger and bigger as the days went by. Surely no one's that committed to a joke.

The harder things got to manage, the more Ose took care of

her too. And she certainly needed the care. A few months later she went to the hospital. Two children emerged during labour. The Irish midwife didn't think the poor woman was done quite just yet. She insisted there was another baby. How merciless. But she was right. My best friend Ose soon had three new siblings. Three new brothers. His mother had just given birth to triplets.

I still remember how excited and shocked the entire hostel was. All the residents were looking forward to meeting their small and new fellow residents even though it meant they had to live under the same oppressive system. The system of Direct Provision. It was all over the local press too. It's funny that I still remember that. One day, after seeing his mother and the babies in the Munster Express I looked at Ose and said, "Your mother's famous." In a way she was, I guess. Well, what a way to learn about the miracle of childbirth.

Things weren't the same after that. Ose and his mother lived in the same room even with the family doubling. They were not given any more space. On the rare occasions where I would visit him, he had his hands full. There was always so much noise. The room was full of life. The thick walls tried to contain it. I wished they could be free. So did he.

I remember thinking selfishly about now I had less time with my best friend now. We grew more distant. Not by choice but by consequence. The knocks on door 39 grew rare. I spent a lot more time on my own. But eventually he came back. Or perhaps I came back. Things fell into a routine, and we had time for each other again. He couldn't have been older than seven, and yet he had adult responsibilities. Looking at him I learned early on about the hardships that were to come my way. He taught me how to face them. How to have patience. Not on purpose. But he did. Without him realizing. Without me realizing. He had inspired me. We were running around again, chasing each other. Helping each other with our homework. Watching TV together. Then one day I heard a familiar knock. It was Ose. Ready to walk out the door to play like every other day I quickly realized that today wasn't like every other day. "I'm moving."

Old luggage and big plump bin bags overran his room. All his belongings were ready for the move. I didn't know exactly where County Meath was then, but I knew that it was far. Too far. My mother took me out to buy sweets for him. A goodbye present. We hugged. That was it.

The night before he left, I went to the bathroom and cried. I was about to turn seven soon. I can never forget that night. I had never cried for a friend before. I had never cried for a departure before. This was new. He was gone before I awoke. The person I shared everything with. The only person I believed understood me. My one friend. My family. He was gone. I was late for school that day. It was the worst day of childhood and unfortunately, it would be on repeat for the next ten years.

A part of me hopes that he remembers me. But a more merciful part of me prays that he doesn't. That is not the childhood he deserved. It is not one any child deserved. Ose, my best friend.

The days went by. I grew older. What was once new and unusual became normal. I had come to accept that this hostel was my home. Even if it never felt like it. It's where I must exist. The notion of ever leaving grew more and more foreign. It was hard to make local Irish friends. I couldn't invite them over. That wasn't allowed. Not that they would want to anyway, and I certainly don't blame them. Residents couldn't even leave for the night without getting permission. Without noting down every detail of why, where, with whom they were leaving. There was no concept of privacy or dignity. We were stripped of all independence.

However, the older I got the more I wanted to learn about myself. Not in a conscious way. But I was curious. Who was I? I always loved to tell stories. I always loved to write. I wanted to be an artist, a creator of some kind. I knew that somehow.

One day there was a knock on door 39. It was a woman. She was white. She had a headscarf. "I'm giving some of the kids art lessons, just for fun," she told my mother. "Was that an American accent?" How odd, I remember thinking. But here was a fellow resident here who was just willing to share some time and knowledge with children she didn't know.

I had never painted before. Walking into a common room, I saw that she had her own personal materials all laid out on a table. She let us use them. I painted for the first time. I remember feeling happy. It was rare. I remember the strong smell of the acrylic paint as it soaked into the paintbrush. I loved it.

She was kind. She had wisdom. I remember being in awe. Who was this person? One day she was painting a mural in the small, bare "playroom." Snow White and the seven dwarfs. She captured each dwarf's personality. See I knew this because we had just seen the Disney classic at school not so long before. I was mesmerized. I had never seen someone paint like that. She had also painted a mural inside her room that she shared with two other women. She got in trouble for that one.

We talked a lot. I was barely eight, but she treated me with respect. She talked about my talent. My ability. I had never had conversations like that before. I had never had an adult friend before. I had never seen such kindness before. She told me how much she wanted to travel. How much she wanted to experience new things. She said she loved different cultures and traditions. Oh, and especially food. She loved Indian food. Apparently, she had been there before and longed to go back sometime. So, one day to say thank you my mother made her a special dish.

Residents weren't allowed to cook of course but my mother had been here long enough to learn the tricks necessary to survive. She was a traditional Pakistani mother. Nothing was going to stop her from cooking for her kids. She had acquired a hotplate from a local charity shop. It was hidden under the bed in our room so that it wouldn't be taken away during a surprise inspection. They happened often enough. All our drawers and closets were checked. If anything was closed it was opened and examined. The exact reason for this still eludes me. Something about our own safety. Yes, I'm sure that's true.

Well, my mother made a special red lentil soup or dal served over fragrant basmati rice. She added some pickled vegetables or achar on the side. My new art teacher hadn't had a meal like this for a while, and I was happy to surprise her with it. She couldn't travel, but that didn't mean her tastebuds couldn't. She loved it. Almost as much as I loved her classes. They became my favourite part of living. For at least a few months. Then one day she was gone. I didn't say goodbye. Neither did she. But it was the end of that. No more art classes. No more expressing myself. It was all over. I would never meet her again. I don't know where she went. I didn't even know her name. Or at least I don't remember it.

I did learn that she was Jewish. Is that important? I was a young Muslim boy. And even then, somehow, I found that it was important. In some way. It meant something. I didn't know what, but I loved it. It felt unique to this place. A silver lining perhaps to an otherwise inhumane system. She didn't just teach me about art. She didn't just let me use her paint. She taught me about life. About ambition. About hope. About myself. She was my friend. My oldest friend yet. My art teacher.

Seasons change. The hostel changes. Not the suffocating rules. But the people. They make up the landscape. And the landscape was always changing, I was beginning to get used to departures. That's what I told myself anyway. As time went by I moved on from one class to another. I moved from one school to another. Yes, entering second class in the Green School. I felt so old. Although I hadn't even turned nine yet. It had been years now. You can really grow accustomed to injustice. And I had. That's what makes it so dangerous. Inequality was the default way of life. I wasn't fighting it. My mother was fighting that battle on her own. Then one day a new family moved in. All the way from Iran. There was a son. He was my age. I remember smiling when my mother told me that.

Reza. It didn't take long for us to bond. I gave him a quick tour of the place. We didn't zoom up and down and across the halls. I had since refined my methods of giving hostel tours. I was much older now. A new family coming in was always bittersweet. There was hope that I could make new friends. But the realisation that a whole new family were going to be introduced to an oppressive system under which they'd have to live certainly put a damper on things. But Reza was optimistic. When we first met, he was very shy. He seemed introverted. Like I was on my first day. But it wasn't long before he was knocking on my door every morning. Like all my friends prior.

He had these large round glasses. They almost covered half of his face. He had a large imagination too. For a building constantly being filled and removed of children, that commodity actually seemed rare enough. He lived on the ground floor. That part of the floor had remained empty for so long. After being refurbished it was ready to house new, hopeful residents. It smelled like a hospital. I hated going down there. So, he would always come up, asking to play.

Play. I didn't really do that for a while. But when Reza came in, he brought a spark. A new air. Something my lungs desperately needed. Like with friends before, we did everything together. He became integral to my world. An extension of my life. But for the first time, I felt like a real child. My imagination was being reinstalled. And it was all because of him. We used to watch so many cartoons together. Especially anything with superheroes. I had watched cartoons before of course, but they never really took a hold on me before. Not in this way. Then one day when he called at my room and dragged me outside, he told me, "We're going to make our own show!" Yes, our own TV series. Where we would be the stars. Superpowers and all. That's how *The Adventures of Firebot and Agent Rain* began.

I was a fire summoning robot, and he was a top-secret agent that could bend water. We would team up together to save the hostel from some very unusually regular paranormal, extraterrestrial threats. While a film crew filmed us of course. I was young, but even still found it too childish, to begin with. But before I knew it, we were already halfway through a season. He would call for me at room 39 every day during late spring that year, and we would go off on our adventures just as the sun was setting. For the first time in a very long time, I was having fun. Real fun. Because I let myself forget. The pain of being where I was. The uncertainty of my future. The sorrow growing within my mother as the days went by. I had forgotten how important imagination was. Or perhaps I never knew to begin with. But Reza made me realise how badly I needed it. I needed to escape. And he taught me how.

A few months had passed, and another child came to live in Bridgewater House. He was from Ethiopia and was a year younger than both Reza and me. He moved into the room opposite Reza's on the ground floor. We quickly became friends, but as time went on it became clear that their close proximity allowed their bond to grow stronger. Eventually, Reza started knocking less and less on my door. We didn't shoot as many episodes of our show as we once used to. But it was okay. We needed a break anyway. Right?

I definitely felt jealous though. We began to drift further and further apart. Then one day it seemed the entire hostel was absorbed by some recent news. The entire ground floor was being relocated. Every resident on it was being moved. I had seen departures before but not on such a grand scale. An entire floor. Perhaps Reza and I growing apart was some sort of divine mercy. It won't hurt as much now that he is leaving. Unexpectedly, the evening before he was to go, he knocked on my door for the final time. "Do you want to shoot one final episode?" he asked excitedly. Of course, I did. And we both ran outside and fought our final battle. The hostel was safe now and forever.

His move came at the end of summer. Exactly on the day that I was to return to school. However, I convinced my mother to let me be late so that I could stay to say goodbye. It didn't take much convincing. She had seen many of my disappointments before and didn't have the heart to not let me have this one moment. A large white bus arrived right outside the big black gates of the hostel. As all the residents lined up to take their seats, I gave my friend Reza one final hug.

An end to another friendship. But I was stronger now. Perhaps desensitized to the misery of losing loved ones. Reza and his neighbour both were being moved to the same hostel far away. They both excitedly entered the bus and sat together as they waved at me through the window. Yes, I guess it was getting easier. Then as Reza's mother came by and gave me a hug, I inexplicably burst into tears. What was this? I thought I had gotten over loss. I guess I wasn't as strong as I thought. Reza seemed surprised to see me cry through the window. That was the last time he saw me and the last time I saw him. I wish I could have been stronger but at least he knew that he was important.

Life would have been much more difficult for me had I not learned how to imagine. How to escape this world and into one that is more just, more equal. A world that made more sense. Even if it included flaming robots. And I have Reza to thank for that. Sometimes my family catches me talking to myself. Understandably they think it's odd. Little do they know that I'm keeping *The Adventures of Firebot and Agent Rain* alive. Although I've long lost count of what episode I'm on.

I don't think I understood then just how much I had learned. How much I was learning. Years went by. I aged with them. Ten, eleven, twelve, and so on. I had forgotten that this was temporary. Now it was just where I lived. Any other way of life seemed unusual. But every resident around me was teaching me something. Whether they knew it or not. Whether I knew it or not.

More kids came in of course. There was a child named Reggie from the Democratic Republic of the Congo. Another child, Nadir, from my own home country of Pakistan moved into the same floor as mine. The knocking on my room began once more. And I was grateful for it.

One particular afternoon, Nadir and Reggie decided to have a race. Down from the big black gates towards the main door of the hostel, which was within the conservatory. Nadir had picked up too much speed sprinting down the slope and couldn't deaccelerate successfully enough. He shattered through the conservatory glass window. There was glass everywhere. But there wasn't a scratch on him. He was fine. And laughing. And so was I. More than I had ever done before. We were in pretty big trouble, but I needed that. I need to laugh.

On another evening Nadir and Reggie knocked on my door like they always did before. But this time they had planned something. On this occasion, all three of us snuck into the basement of the hostel. We weren't allowed down there but we had already been there before. There was this one big wooden door down there that we always wondered about. A grand mystery of the building. Where did it lead? What kind of secrets was it hiding? We were always too afraid to open it though. We were not allowed to be anywhere close to it. We could only imagine the trouble we'd be in if we actually entered it. But that one evening Reggie and Nadir were determined to have it open. They wanted me to do it.

With my hand on the rusty metal handle, I could feel my heartbeat. I would usually never do this. But they were right behind me, with faith that I could. And then after taking a deep breath, I pushed the door out. A loud ringing tore through the basement. We all realized that the door was attached to an alarm. Both Nadir and Reggie ran as if their lives depended on it. I was about to leg it too but not before I could quickly take in what was behind that door. To my disappointment, it was just the outside world. The door opened up to the main street of the little town of Carrick. The outside. I guess in a way, although not a secret, it was kept hidden from me. Locked behind doors and guarded by alarm systems. Just another reminder of who I was and where I was. No freedom for me just yet.

But I felt happy that I did it. The manager was anything but happy as she later reviewed the security footage. We were forced to apologize. But I was grateful. I felt some sort of satisfaction from breaking the rules. I had been locked behind the wall of that building for years. It felt like a God-given right for me to know what every door led to. So, if wanted to open the damn door I was going to open it.

For so long, that part of me that wanted to be brave and daring was lost. But now I was happy to explore and discover even if meant being a disturbance. Everything in my life was disturbed so why not throw caution to the wind. I felt alive again. And it was my friends who were responsible for that. For showing me that it's okay to break the rules. It's okay to make mistakes. It's okay to be bold.

It wasn't long before Nadir and Reggie left. At this point I really was numb. Or perhaps just accepting. Years and years had gone by, and it felt like my life was on repeat. How often can the sad ending of a movie make you cry anyway? It's just the way it was.

I had moved from primary school to secondary school. At this point, I wasn't really aware of who was coming and going as I just pretty much kept to myself in my room. Went to school, did my homework, did some writing and some drawing watched some tv and then went to bed. That was life. Behind the four walls of direct provision. Watching my mother's hope slowly decay was hard. But that was becoming part of usual life too.

Then came the day when I was to depart. It was unusual. Ten-and-a-half years went by. This was the only childhood I had known. It was the only way of life I had known. But now I was leaving too. We were finally allowed to live in this country. As free citizens. Why it took them so long to decide is beyond me. But I was happy. Because my mother needed this. Late? Sure, but still necessary. We were free.

Just as we had come, we were leaving carrying our luggage up the driveway towards the gates. 2005 to 2015. Five to sixteen. Yes, this was unusual. The world I had come into was not the world I was leaving. Every face that I saw as a mystified child entering those gates no longer lived there to bid me adieu. The entire landscape had changed. For better. Or for worse. As the big black gates closed behind me for the very last time, I didn't hear the usual creaking.

I heard footsteps zooming up the stairs. I heard the bristles of a paintbrush sweeping across the wall. I heard the crying and laughter of newborns. Yes, all three. I heard the storm summoned by Agent Rain and the blaze erupting from Firebot's mechanical arms. I heard the sound of glass shattering and the endless ringing of a high-pitched alarm.

Most of all I heard the knocking on room 39. Every knock taught me something. Every knock shaped me into who I am. Every knock expressed a friendship. The start of one as well as the end. An introduction and a departure. Who would I be if weren't for those who knocked? I can't say. Ten years of knocking and every knock made a difficult life more bearable.

So, to all those who knocked on room 39. Thank you.

Rose Ngatchou

A Summer Point of View

"Walk with me," said Ms. Mary as soon as I arrived on site. I was a junior camp counselor at Little Friends for Peace, and it was my first day. "We have this girl," she continued, "She needs a translator—correction, she needs you."

I was confused and wondered why she thought that I would be fit for such a task. I wasn't the only French speaker there and, in comparison to them, my French could have used more work. Ms. Mary stopped walking, and I followed suit. That was when I saw her: a small, frail, girl with braided hair and a lost expression.

"Bonjour?" She asked, unsure of whether or not I would be able to understand her. "*Bonjour, je m'appelle Rose*," I responded. Relief replaced the confused gaze on her face. With that, the director was satisfied, "So, you can be her personal counselor for the week?" She asked, beaming. I blinked blankly. This was something very new to me. I didn't know if I could help her. But, I knew that I could try. I caught another glimpse as she looked around the room. I searched for something in her eyes. How was she feeling? Did she want to be here? I analyzed the African print on the fabric she was wearing and wondered where was she from?

"If you believe that I'm the best person to do this, then I am more than willing to, Ms. Mary," I responded, looking away from the girl.

"Yes! I'll give you both time to introduce yourselves. Thank you, Rose!"

With that, she walked away, leaving me alone with the little girl. For a moment, we didn't say anything, but I broke the silence. I learned as much about her as I could. Her name was Esther. She was from Mali. My eyes lit up when she told me because I had worked at their Embassy. I couldn't wait to share with her what I had learned from my time there. Her favorite color was purple, and she had arrived in the U.S just two weeks before. She explained to me that her family told her to pack her stuff the day they were supposed to leave. And that of all her toys she was only able to salvage a doll. With that, we headed back to the morning circle, and my day of translating began.

Esther was hilarious! I was one of the few people she could talk to, so we shared a lot. I taught her how to introduce herself to the other campers, and helped them communicate with her in return. I even used the camp activities to help teach her English phrases. She helped me with my Bambara, her native language. And, taught me something about people, indirectly. I felt her becoming more engaged in the activities and was touched to be a witness of her growth. Before our last day of camp, I had been encouraging Esther to participate in the final performance of our group's play. She was nervous at first but agreed. Not only did she master her English lines, but she taught everyone in our group some French! At the end, I gave her a box to open.

"*Mais, ce boxe pèse. Il y a quoi dedans*?" She asked me.

"Open it," I said, smiling. Inside was an assortment of all kinds of toys, but mostly dolls.

We were from different parts of the continent. We had different religions, different points of view, and different customs. But there was something we shared in common: a language. I learned that this is what connects us all. Because like Esther, people just want to be understood. Using my French to translate probably meant more to me than her. In French, I find the connecter that links my identities. In language, I find more than just words. I find people.

Deirdre Hutchison

Feeling I Didn't Belong, I Wanted to Hide in My Phone

What could be the connection between Lowell and Cork in the current climate? Many living in the United States or Ireland are well aware of the links between the two countries—shaped by a long history of migration and interaction. But to me as a Cork native and now a student at the University of Massachusetts Lowell, this connection is a link to my past, my present and my future.

My journey to the present began more than three decades ago when I left my homeland behind. Like millions before me, I was looking for a new life. Born and raised in the suburbs of Cork, I enjoyed all the fruits of a rich and diverse secondary-level education system. But, I must confess, those sentiments are now from my adult perspective. As a teen, I was far less enamored with the life of Peig Sayers or Pythagoras's theorem; however, I applied myself and did well in high school until my world began to unravel at fourteen years old. Shortly after experiencing headaches and flashes of light in my vision, I woke one day completely blind in my left eye. A few weeks in hospital gave way to weekly visits for hours of testing to reach a diagnosis. Ongoing symptoms prevented full participation in academics resulting in a downward spiral. After many months, I regained ninety-five percent of my vision—although a reoccurrence years later left me with thirty percent permanent blindness in that eye. However, within eighteen months of my initial symptoms, my stepfather, the only father I had ever known, died of cancer. These tumultuous events rocked my world and further challenged my capacity to participate in my academics. When I received my Leaving Certificate results, I passed only four of the required five exams. I failed. I did not graduate high school. Failing the Leaving Certificate earned a certain stigma. In my mind, I was a failure and had the records to prove it: shame and embarrassment were my constant companions.

My options were limited. College was only viable if I went back and repeated the school year. I already knew I wasn't smart enough the first time around, and I would not risk further humiliation by a second failure. So, when my mum moved to England my final year of high school, I quickly made my escape following in her heels. Knowing my limitations without high school qualifications, I valued my temporary job placement and worked extremely hard. Fear can hinder or help in many situations, and in this scenario, it helped develop a strong work ethic that has served me well. As time progressed, I pursued opportunities within the corporate environment and maintained a respectable career. My penchant for traveling brought my husband and me to the United States. We eventually settled in Massachusetts as other family members had already made the leap. With two young children to raise, one with special needs, I was both busy and happy—for the most part. Despite my successes, I always felt deeply insecure about my lack of education. Now I was living in a country and interacting with people who predominantly had a college education.

My feelings of inadequacy mounted. Countless times since I left school, the same nightmare would occur with a teacher asking me the answer to a math problem—it's always a math problem—and all I can do is sit there, silently crumbling inside because I have no idea of the answer. It is not an understatement to say my academic insecurities plagued me. I dreamed of going to college. I dreamed of having a degree. I dreamed of being smart. Somehow my fear still held me back until one day; I got tired of being afraid. I witnessed my mum on her college journey as a mature student and decided to do whatever it would take, however long it needed, but I would go to college. So, after some refresher courses at a local community college, I tentatively stepped onto the campus of the University of Massachusetts, Lowell, to pursue a Bachelor of Arts in History.

I came for the academics, and after taking almost thirty college classes, I am discovering a world I never knew existed. There is no denying how thrilling it was exploring the rich account of Ibn Battuta's travels, what shaped Mary Rowlandson's biased toward Native Americans, or the prevalence of homosexuality within the monarchy in medieval England—of course, not forgetting Herodotus, the founding father of historical scholarship. What I did not anticipate, however, was how much I would learn about myself beyond academics.

I could fill a book with examples of how many positive experiences I have had at university. Still, two come to mind that dramatically changed my thinking and positively influenced my success at college. As indicated earlier, my academic insecurities were deeply ingrained. Writing absolutely terrified me, so I avoided it whenever I could. Unfortunately, College Writing I & II provided no escape. On my first day of class, my professor announced that people were not born good writers; nobody saw the fifteen or twenty edits a piece went through before completion. Good writers worked on their papers, and anyone could be a good writer. All it needed was effort and dedication. I was flooded with relief, but more importantly, I was given hope. Even I could learn to write a good paper. Truthfully, as I share this account, it has brought tears to my eyes. Remembering where I am coming from with such paralyzing fear of writing and seeing how far I have come. I am under no illusion that I will ever become a Pulitzer Prize-winning author, but I am confident that I can write. I can write research papers, academic essays, lighthearted blog posts, professional applications; the list is endless. Today, I do those with newfound confidence. Some anxiety still creeps in, but it quickly fades as I start each new project.

One other occasion that altered my thought process significantly occurred very early on in college. In my late forties at the time, I was invariably the oldest in the class. My classmates were my daughter's age, and I felt I had nothing in common. Once again, my insecurities arose, and my vulnerability was all-consuming. Feeling I didn't belong, I wanted to hide in my phone just like my classmates as we sat in a circle waiting for the professor. Suddenly I found the courage to speak up and ask a student if they found the homework as challenging as I had. I was willing to be vulnerable. The floodgates opened, and many chimed in, sharing their homework experiences and how awkward it felt not knowing anyone. We had a commonality, and we bonded. Despite my pride, I discovered it was okay to be vulnerable, I am not unique, and good things can come from uncomfortable situations. These examples underscore the level of acceptance and support I have received at UMass Lowell. It has given me a voice. Although academics were all I expected from college, I am humbled by how much I am learning about myself and life beyond textbooks. Today, I view my education as integrated rather than compartmentalized, an area where I am pushed emotionally and intellectually to reach for my dreams, especially those I didn't know I had.

My education began in Cork, a city I am proud always to call home. As I get closer to attaining my degree in a city almost 3,000 miles away, I am equally proud to call UMass Lowell home. It may seem like the end of my journey, but I feel it is just the beginning.

Contributors

Corkman **Pat Brett** studied Electrical Engineering at University College Cork before moving to Finance with PwC and finally (for now!) Musgrave, where he is Head of Supply Chain Performance. Whilst many left Cork after graduating, to come back later, Pat took the shortcut and never left. Father to four Inspirations, downtime is mostly spent on the touchline cheering them on whilst wishing he was out there too. After a positive response from a small audience for his occasional in-house blogging at work, he decided to test the authenticity of colleague feedback on his musings by making this submission to *Atlantic Currents II*.

Alan Egan is a native of Cork City. He continues to be fascinated by Cork's diverse history, and by the array of characters who daily walk its streets. After a long career in the financial world, he became a fulltime student at University College Cork and, having completed both a primary and master's degree, he was a tutor there for a number of years. During this time, he began to write family and local history articles and in 2016 he tried his hand at fiction. Alan's work has been published in the *Holly Bough* (2014), *Matador and Other Short Stories* (2018), I*reland's Own Short Story Anthology* (2019 and 2021), *The Same Page Anthology (2021)* and *Arís Times* (2021).

John FitzGerald's first full-length poetry collection *The Time Being* was published by Gallery Press in 2021. He has published two letterpress editions with The Salvage Press, *Haiku na Feirme* (2022) and *Darklight* (2019). His pamphlet, *First Cut* was published in 2017 by Southword Editions, in their New Irish Voices Series. His poems have appeared in journals, newspapers, and anthologies. He has won the Patrick Kavanagh Prize and was shortlisted for a Hennessy New Irish Writing Award. He lives with his family on a farm in County Cork and works at University College Cork as University Librarian.

James McKeon is a seventy-nine-year-old Irish writer/actor/poet/artist with more than twenty plays and books to his name, best known is *Frank O'Connor—A Life*. Winner of awards in Ireland, Japan, Germany, and the USA, he has lectured on O'Connor at University College Cork, Ireland, and the USA. He has been a guest on *The Late Late Show* three times. He lives in Cork with his wife, Margaret.

Aisling Twomey was born and raised in Cork city and attended University College Cork where she graduated with a BCl (Hons) and LLM (Criminal Justice). Her journalism has been published in *The Irish Times, Irish Examiner, Irish Independent*, and others. She graduated from Birkbeck, University of London, with an MA in Creative Writing in 2020. Aisling was longlisted for the Spread the Word Life Writing Prize in 2019. Other writing has appeared in *Headstuff* and *yolk*. She lives in London with her boyfriend and a very cheeky dog.

Bill Williams completed an MSc in Chemistry at University College Cork in 1973 and went on to work in education in Ireland, UK, Eritrea, Kenya, Mozambique, and Portugal and to run distance courses for the International Labour Organization in various African lusophone countries. Based in Portugal since 1989, he is a member of the Engineering Management and

Management Science Research Centre at IST, University of Lisbon, and is Adjunct Senior Research Fellow at TUDublin, Ireland. He was lead editor of *Engineering Practice in a Global Context, Understanding the Technical and the Social,* an edited volume published by Routledge in 2014. While he has published extensively in the field of engineering education, this is his first literary publication.

Róisín Leggett Bohan wakes at five and plays with words while the house sleeps. Her work has appeared in *New Irish Writing* and various journals and anthologies. She has been shortlisted for competitions including the Allingham, Gloucestershire, and Hammond House prize and was awarded a Poetry Mentoring Fellowship from the Munster Literature Centre in 2021. Róisín is a recipient of an Arts Council of Ireland Award, is co-creator of The Same Page Anthology and holds an MA (Hons) in creative writing from University College Cork. Her work often explores the theme of loss and the courage that lies within vulnerability. Visit www.inkstainedwings.com if you would like to know more.

Tadhg Carey was born in Ireland in November 1959. He entered University College Cork as an undergraduate student in 1978 but, due to family circumstances beyond his control, Tadhg was forced to leave UCC before graduating. He joined the petroleum industry in 1981. Six years later Tadhg embarked on a twenty-eight-year career as an innovator and company CEO in petroleum training and online learning. With three adult children from his previous marriage, Tadhg and his partner Tanya have a seven-year-old son. His unquenchable passion since childhood has been writing and storytelling, and finally, after a forty-year absence, he returned to UCC in 2018 to study English. Tadhg has recently completed his first fantasy novel (as yet unpublished) and he has also commenced writing the second instalment of this series.

Sonja Murphy completed her BA in English at University College Cork last year. She is studying for a master's in modern English

Literature at UCC, while also working part-time at a bookshop. During her undergraduate degree, she was a member of UCC's English society and part of the editing team for its literary journal, *The Quarryman*. In her free time, she loves to write, paint, and walk her dog.

Margaret O'Driscoll lives in Cobh where she writes memoir and poetry. In 2021, she completed a Master's in Creative Writing at University College Cork, and is working towards her first poetry collection. Her poems have been published in various journals. She self-published a memoir on the strong women in her husband's family.

Rehan Ali is a writer and filmmaker. Originally from Pakistan, he arrived in Ireland in 2005 at the age of six. He is a Neuroscience graduate currently pursuing a Master's in Bioinformatics and Computational Biology at University College Cork. It was while growing up in the small town of Carrick-on-Suir, Co. Tipperary that Rehan fell in love with storytelling. This love for writing eventually grew into a passion for film. He hopes to further bring to light through the medium of film the conversations and concerns of the very diverse community within which he grew.

Bill O'Connell has been living in the Pioneer Valley in Massachusetts since 1984. A retired social worker, he teaches writing at Greenfield Community College and runs a small handyman business. Books of poetry include *Sakonnet Point* (Plinth Books, 2011), *On the Map to Your Life* (Dytiscid Press 1992), and *When We Were All Still Alive* (Open Field Press, 2022) from which the poems "I Asked Her to Sing the Oldest Song She Knew," "Solo," "When We Were All Still Alive," and "Luke" are reprinted with permission of the author.

Christine O'Connor is completing a collection of literary-themed essays, as well as a memoir on her grandmother and the *Titanic*. Much of her writing has connections to Ireland. She is a co-editor of *Trasna*, an online platform featuring writing from Ireland. A former board member of the Henry David Thoreau Society, this past summer she presented a paper at its annual gathering: "In a Lake of Rainbow Light: Where Thoreau and the Irish Meet." She holds an MA in American Studies from Boston College, a JD from Suffolk University, and serves as chief legal counsel for the city of Lowell, Massachusetts.

Phil Terrana grew up in Rochester, New York, and has lived in Virginia Beach, Virginia, since 1978. He served in Vietnam as a writer for the 1st Aviation Brigade's *HAWK* magazine after graduating from Lowell Technological Institute in 1969. He's always found the newspaper editorial page to be a better barometer of public opinion than most opinion polls and continues to send articles to newspapers. He's been a Guest Columnist at *The Virginian-Pilot*. Since retiring from the Postal Service in 2010, he's published five novels, the latest being *The Life, Times & Adventures of Hoag Franklin*, and recently a collection of short stories entitled *Giving Ideas a Voice & Room to Grow*. He enjoys traveling, reading, and spending time with his family.

Deirdre Hutchison was born and raised in Cork but emigrated to the UK aged 18. Ten years later she moved to California for two years. She moved to Massachusetts next and has resided there for almost twenty years. Deirdre is a senior at the University of Massachusetts Lowell pursuing a BA degree. She is majoring in History and minoring in Medieval Studies. Her honors college project is a study on Warren K. Moorehead. Her first article, "Do they have traffic lights in Ireland?" was published by the *American Studies Blog* of the American Studies Journal. In her free time, Deirdre likes to travel, visit museums, and spend time with her family.

Rosalie Ngatchou is a sophomore at UMass Lowell. Some of her favorite things to do are writing in her journal, watching movies, reading, and listening to music. She has a huge love for storytelling, communicating, and connecting with other people. She believes that we are all connected in some way and through nurturing and keeping our connections open, we can create a more compassionate world.

Emily Rios was born and raised in Lowell, Massachusetts. She's always found comfort in the natural world, and the Merrimack River provides for her in difficult times. She is not interested in any one thing; her creativity drives her passion for literature, graphic design, vegan cooking, and much more. She is an afternoon arts instructor, working two jobs to support her family while earning a degree in English literature. Despite challenges, she believes that the natural world and a creative spirit can inspire great change.

Margaret Tseng has been fascinated by the written word since fourth grade, when they wrote a picture book which was sewn and illustrated by hand. They grew up in Medford, Mass., where they walked to high school uphill both ways. They are an author of poetry, short essays, and nonfiction articles. Currently, they are studying physics at UMass Lowell. In their free time, they enjoy hiking, solving puzzles, and writing code for increasingly obscure and unusual purposes.

Paul Marion is co-editor of the original *Atlantic Currents* and author of the poetry collections *Lockdown Letters* and *Union River.*

John Wooding is the author of *The Power of Non-Violence: The Enduring Legacy of Richard Gregg* and co-editor of the original *Atlantic Currents: Connecting Cork and Lowel*l.

Prizewinners

UML ALUMNI FIRST PRIZE

Bill O'Connell
(multiple poems)

SECOND PRIZE

Christine O'Connor:
Annie's Bike, Brian Friel, And Translating Loss

Phil Terrana:
Never Mess With a Nun Named Leo

UML STUDENTS FIRST PRIZE

Deirdre Hutchinson:
Feeling I Didn't Belong, I Wanted to Hide in My Phone

SECOND PRIZE

Rosalie Ngatchou:
A Summer Point of View

Emily Rios:
The River

Margaret Tseng:
Going to the Woods

UCC ALUMNI FIRST PRIZE

John FitzGerald:
The Island

SECOND PRIZE

Pat Brett:
Things I Would Have Told You in the Canteen

Bill Williams:
Chimoio

Alan Egan:
An Extraordinary Man

Aisling Twomey:
Hometown Legacy

James McKeon:
The Promise

UCC STUDENTS FIRST PRIZE

Roísín Bohan:
Everything Possible Happens Somewhere

Tadhg Carey:
Standing in the Dome Of Hades

Margaret O'Driscoll:
Moondancing in the Bay of Biscay

Rehan Ali:
Those Who Knocked on Room 39

Sonja Murphy:
Jumping Back in Time